~

CHECK IT OUT!

~

COMMUNICATIONS AND MEDIA STUDIES SERIES
Robin Andersen, series editor

CHECK IT OUT!

~

Great Reporters on What It Takes to Tell the Story

~

Art Athens

Fordham University Press
New York
2004

Communications and Media Studies Series, No. 11
ISSN 1522-385X

LIBRARY OF CONGRESS CATALOGING-IN-PUBLICATION DATA

Athens, Art.
    CHECK IT OUT! : great reporters on what it takes to tell the story / Art Athens. — 1st ed.
    p. cm. — (Communications and media studies series; no. 11)
Includes index.
ISBN 0-8232-2352-3 (hardcover) — ISBN 0-8232-2353-1 (pbk.)
    1. Television broadcasting of news—United States. 2. Journalism—United States. I. Title. II. Communications and media studies; no. 11.
PN4888.T4A84 2004
070.4'3'0973—dc22   2004018983

Printed in the United States of America
08 07 06 05 04   5 4 3 2 1
First edition

DEDICATION—

To my family, as they rode the reportorial roller coaster at my side: the cancelled dates, the interrupted dinners, the calls in the middle of the night, the calls in the middle of the day, the fourteen-hour crashing deadlines, the weekend work, the nighttime work, the seven-days-a-week work. A special thanks to the overworked, stretched-too-thin, always-on-the-go, always-on-a-deadline correspondents who generously gave of their time so I could tell you what they told me about being excellent. They are.

TABLE OF CONTENTS

ACKNOWLEDGMENTS—

Thank you to Ken Ackerman, president, Broadcast Legends; Van Emberg; Kevin Goldman; H. Paul Jeffers; Mike Ludlum, professor of broadcast journalism, New York University; Don Maxton; Vita West Muir; Eric Newton, managing editor, Newseum; Eric Ober; Bob Priddy; Joan Roth; Jack Swanson, operations manager, KGO; Dr. Vernon Stone, journalism professor emeritus, University of Missouri; Andie Tucher, professor of journalism history, Columbia University Graduate School of Journalism; and my many bosses over the years, who showed me how to do things right and how to do things wrong.

~Preface~

Everywhere you go you hear bad things about the news. At parties. In the office. On the street. Everyone complains about the news. It's too graphic. It's too superficial. It's too boring. It's too biased. Almost never do you hear people say, "I think they do a great job broadcasting the news."

My friends who are still toiling in the journalism game tell me I'm lucky to be out of it. On the contrary, I think I was lucky to have been in it. Sure there are lots of things wrong with it. I have a long list of pet peeves, among them:

- teases that don't deliver
- stories with no substance
- "team" coverage (as if we care how they get along)
- "live" coverage (as opposed to what? Dead coverage? I find the content of much "live" coverage dead anyway.)
- incorrect use of words (for example, anecdote instead of antidote)
- news as entertainment: "The latest survivor to be kicked off the island: live and exclusive, at eleven."
- reporters broadcasting "live" at night from a scene where something happened hours before. There's no reason to be there any longer, and you can't see anything anyway.
- bad grammar
- hyper-hyped news stories that don't live up to their promotion
- cute chatter between anchors (though I do like cute anchors between chatter)
- comments like "Isn't that tragic?" or "What a horrible story."
- ads nauseum

And that's just for starters. Yet, despite all of this, I am still proud of what many of my colleagues and I were able to achieve in broadcast news. We knew how to find great stories and how to recognize great stories when we found them. I also am proud of the level of excellence we achieved, a quality that was once the goal of every news organization.

Ask a physician what is wrong with health care today and he is likely to tell you it's HMOs, poorly trained nurses, politicians interfering, and patients not responding properly to treatment. He is not likely to tell you there's a problem with physicians, the American Medical Association, or the people who run hospitals (and control hospital privileges for physicians).

Ask a highly successful and still active television executive, journalist, or producer what is wrong with their industry and they'll often tell you they're just doing what the public wants, it's a sign of the times, they're just keeping in tune with the culture, it has to be done this way. They will not resort to quoting Pogo, who said (through writer Walt Kelly), "We have found the enemy and it is us." Yet, ironically, industry insiders do not quibble with the central, and widely held, idea—that there is a lot wrong with television news.

In any case, this is why you will find unattributed quotes and comments throughout this book. Some quotes are just left to hang there, and you will have to take them at face value. Others will be apparent in their failure to identify the person speaking or being spoken about. There is, sadly, a need for this anonymity.

Some still-working producers whom I have known for years as friends and colleagues refused to even broach the subject of what really goes on in major newsrooms. It is not that anything terrible happens; it is that they fear that if anyone suspects that they are even discussing this aspect of the industry with a writer, they will lose their jobs. Such is the lot of today's network news employees.

As for the news executives, many I have questioned spoke in clichés and platitudes. They have found the enemy, and it is not themselves.

I started in this business before fax machines, cell phones, or computers. In 1957, FM radio was something listened to by a handful of classical music fans obsessed with their audio equipment. Car radios didn't even have pushbuttons, and portable radios weighed a lot and used big batteries. We had to use carbon paper to make copies of things, and carry a lot of nickels around so we could call in our stories. We had telephone company "Out of order" signs we would slip over payphone coin slots to keep others from grabbing the phone to file a story before we did. Portable tape machines, if we were lucky enough to have them, were spring-wound affairs, and microphones were the size of baseballs, with the bats attached.

In fact, I once told a class of journalism students that the three most important things to remember when covering a story are "Find the bathroom, find the coffee, find the phone."

Compared with what Edward R. Murrow had to work with, we were in hog heaven. But compared with today's well-equipped newshounds, we were struggling. We just didn't know it. What we did know was, we *loved* it.

I recall a conversation I had with a boss of mine one afternoon. We were two veterans of the news wars, sitting in his office, looking out at the newsroom. "The trouble," he lamented, "is there's just too much bullshit in this business these days."

As usual, I felt compelled to disagree with the boss. "On the contrary," I countered, "there isn't any more bullshit in this business now than there was when we first started out. It's just that, because we've been around longer, our ability to detect it has increased, while our ability to tolerate it has decreased. But," I added, "take a look at those twenty-five-year-old kids out there. They don't think it's bullshit. They think it's great!"

Today's young journalists may be dealing with a different kind of bull than we did, but the good ones love what they're doing just as much.

Although the problems, the constraints on achievement, the level of competency, and, sadly, the desire for quality—particularly on the part of management—may be at a low now, there's always tomorrow.

Will there never be another Shakespeare, Mozart, Hemingway, Murrow, or Cronkite? Will there never be another great symphony written or story told? If we believe that, then a bleak future lies ahead for all of us. I began this book project hoping to learn whether high levels of accomplishment could still be realized in broadcast news. If it is true that we learn from our mistakes, then it must follow that we also learn from our successes and how we achieved them. I hope this book will serve as a road map to the past and future of excellence in broadcast journalism.

~

CHECK IT OUT!

~

I

ALL I EVER WANTED TO BE

~WHAT IT TAKES TO EXCEL~

I waited until I was sure no one was home. She kept it in the hall clos-
et, hidden behind a wall of winter coats. I pulled it out from between
the coats and excitedly rolled it to a spot in front of a full-length mirror. I got my clippings, culled from that day's *New York Herald Tribune*;
stood facing the curved handle of my mother's upright vacuum cleaner;
and intoned in my squeaky nine-year-old voice, "This is Artie Athens
with the latest news." My mother's Hoover was my first microphone.

It was 1948, and even then I knew. This was all I ever wanted to be: a
radio journalist reporting the news. I longed to be able to say, "This is
CBS News" on the air, just as the announcers did when my mother and I
listened to the evening news. This was my dream.

I stuck with that dream, and I made it. I reached the top of my field in
the number one market in the world and got to say "CBS News" a thousand times over. I somehow never doubted I would make it and supposed
that anyone could if they had the right attitude, were good at their craft,
were lucky, and were tireless. Or could they?

Move the clock forward almost fifty years, to my retirement party at
New York City's Gracie Mansion in 1995. A colleague addressed the
crowd about the state of journalism, and what he had to say disturbed me.
Journalism was practically dead, he declared. No good journalists were

coming out of journalism schools, and there was no pool from which to hire anyone who knew anything at all. The news business was going down the tubes.

When it was my turn to speak, I knew I had to challenge that statement. "Surely," I said, "among this very group is a budding Walter Cronkite, Brian Williams, Lynn Sherr, or Mike Wallace—or even, perhaps, an Art Athens or two."

True, the environment of the news business was changing rapidly. The "good old days" were often compared with the current "dark days" of tabloid journalism and profit-driven newsrooms. Yet I knew in my heart that if someone wanted passionately enough to achieve the excellence that was broadcast journalism in its heyday, he or she could do it. But what map could they follow to lead them out of this mire of media-ocrity?

"Go to those who have done it best," I thought. "Talk to the Cronkites, the Wallaces, the Brokaws, the Bradleys, the Hewitts. Find out how *they* did it."

What I discovered was a thread of similarities running through the budding careers of my heroes. Even my own beginnings were a part of this fabric. The way I felt when I hauled out that old Hoover, though I didn't know it at the time, was very much the way Walter Cronkite felt when the journalism bug bit *him*. He was twelve, he told me, and a subscriber to *American Boy* magazine, which ran a series of articles on career choices. Articles about lawyers and mining engineers tempted the young Cronkite. But it was the one about newsmen that intrigued him the most.

> I remember an illustration, a drawing of a fellow in a trench coat with a felt hat and a press pass in the brim of the hat. And that made up my mind . . . I didn't think that was journalism; I thought it was being a newspaperman, a reporter.
>
> But fortunately, I was in a high school that was one of the first in the nation, I suppose, to have a journalism course. And it was taught by a part-time teacher who was an editor in one of the papers in Houston, a fellow named Fred Berney, a wonderful, wonderful teacher, I thought; a natural teacher; a kind of tough-city editor-type guy.

That "natural" teacher was just what Cronkite needed to send him down the right road.

I mean, he could capture your attention, your imagination, constantly holding out the great possibilities in this business that he was hoping to lead you into. He was teaching us very early on the absolute necessity of accuracy, of construction of sentences, the inverted pyramid form we learned in those days, the five W's of the lead: who, what, when, where, and why. And how to build a story and how to research.

Cronkite's mentor became the sponsor of the high school newspaper, and Cronkite became its sports editor, byline and all. That was just the start for an eager Walter Cronkite, who had clearly found his passion.

I was sports editor the first year, managing editor the second year, and editor the third year, and I never looked back. He helped one or two of his favorites get summer jobs at the *Houston Post*. I got a job as kind of an exalted copy boy while I was still in high school, and they permitted me to cover a few nonessential stories, like service club lunches that nobody else was likely to cover anyway. But I ended up getting pieces in the paper. I was the proudest fellow in the world to get on the bus that evening and see somebody reading my story, even though it was only two or three paragraphs.

I knew the same thrill and I knew the drive, the churning in the stomach and the sleepless nights of anticipation. When I was fourteen, I marched into the office of the *Jackson Heights Journal*, a weekly giveaway newspaper published out of a tiny second-story office over the Five and Dime on Eighty-second Street in Jackson Heights, Queens, New York. I wanted to be a reporter so badly, I screwed up my courage and ran up the rickety wooden staircase alongside that Five and Dime, determined to knock on the door, go in, and declare, "Hey, mister, I'm a reporter and I need a job for the summer. Will you hire me?"

The office door reminded me of a pulp novel detective's door. It was dark oak, with a big square of frosted glass. On the glass were stenciled the names of the *Jackson Heights Journal* and the other publications that came out of this office every week: the *Woodside Warbler*, the *Corona Courier*, the *Elmhurst Eagle*, and the *Astoria Atlas*. They constituted a stable of neighborhood giveaway weeklies loaded with advertisements for neighborhood stores that couldn't afford to buy advertising in the big papers, like the *Long Island Star Journal* or the *Herald Tribune*.

The publisher himself seemed to me ancient. He was tall and thin as a twig, with a shock of out-of-control white hair and fingers yellow from the cigarettes he smoked constantly. His office was one large room with a couple of rolltop desks, some wooden chairs, and a few tables. Every horizontal surface was piled high with newspapers, clippings, and old mail.

I regaled him with tales of the eighth-grade newspaper I published at P.S. 69. Two friends and I wrote, typed, mimeographed, and then sold the paper for a nickel a pop. They wouldn't let us sell it in school, though, because of the nature of our stories. We didn't know about checking sources, so we published a lot of rumors about people. We learned our lesson when we were almost expelled after publishing unsubstantiated stories about our eighth-grade teacher and a wig she allegedly wore. The mother of a classmate had told us that our teacher, who was as old as the school itself—perhaps older than the entire educational system of the City of New York—wore a wig. Rumor had it that she would sometimes stick a pencil in her hair, and when she'd reach for it, it would catch on the alleged wig and knock it askew. Well, the story wasn't true, but to young, news-hungry journalists like us it seemed too good *not* to be true. What a story! It made the front page. *We* made the principal's office. It was awful.

Faux pas like this notwithstanding, I was convinced I was a born journalist. Apparently I convinced the *Jackson Heights Journal* publisher, too, for hire me he did. I was his only employee. I had two duties. One was to go through the *big* papers, like the *Long Island Star Journal*, and clip out stories about people or things that involved Corona, Jackson Heights, Astoria, and other neighborhoods his newspapers "covered." I was to separate them into piles; then, using the same two-finger typing style I used throughout my entire career—and in writing this book—I would rewrite the stories so they could legitimately appear in one of the neighborhood weeklies published out of the *Journal* office.

I had one more mandatory duty, which taught me an important lesson about the business and myself. Every morning I would have to walk the ten blocks to the newspaper office, climb those creaky stairs, unlock the big oak door with the big glass panel, and walk the dog.

Yes, in addition to being a publishing magnate, my benefactor was a dog lover. This particular dog, a pug, lived in the office. I think he was older than the boss. He seemed to regret my arrival, because I would wake him up and he would then be faced with going up and down those rickety stairs. But there was a lesson I learned here: I would do absolutely anything to get a chance to be a journalist, even for twenty-five cents an hour. I still remember the thrill I got when that first story I rewrote actually appeared in print, verbatim. It was all worth it.

I also learned early that being a journalist was far from glamorous. Certainly, glamour was the magnet for me then—and, for many, it still is. Walter Cronkite remembers that very thought attracting him when he read the story and looked at the sketch of the reporter in *American Boy*.

> I think it was the indication that this fellow lived a very glamorous life, although "glamour" wasn't a word in any of our lexicons at that time. I think what appealed to me was he worked his way up to foreign correspondent, and here he was traveling around to remote corners of the world. But also, before that, he chased fires and ambulances, and there was a sense of not only a very active participation in life as it was being lived, but that he actually had a part, a role *on the inside*. And I think that probably was the thing that appealed to me most, that you got to know things before anybody else did.

CURIOSITY

When I was a kid and saw a police line with a sign that said, "Do Not Cross," I thought, "Someday I'm gonna cross that line." Ultimately I did. For me, money or success or career was never the goal; it was always about crossing that line. I had a burning curiosity that took hold and wouldn't let go. Walter Cronkite felt it too—that unquenchable compulsion to find things out, capped with the need to tell others what you'd learned. "I think there's some of that," he reflects, "in all successful reporters. One thing that is necessary is a curiosity about even the most mundane things."

Cronkite notes that it's easy to be curious about what goes on behind the scenes in the Oval Office, for example. But the *natural* journalist wonders about little, everyday things as well.

I actually made this investigation, not too long ago, when I was in New York, maybe twenty or thirty years ago. I spent a day in a shoe store . . . because I was interested in how they kept an inventory on all of those shoes. How many shoes were back there? It was a little tiny shoe store, and they went through a little door and somehow came out with an 11B in the color and style I wanted. How could they do that? And how did they know when they sold one or if they had another. And I just got fascinated.

What did Cronkite learn from his investigation?

I found out that they've got a terrible pile of that stuff in the back, and in the old days, before computers, they had a huge pile of papers they were marking off every time they sold a pair.

That drive to find out why, coupled with a need to tell everyone what you found out, has led many a seasoned journalist down a blind alley. Once I discovered I would have to pay $1,200 to fly from New York to San Francisco on Monday and return to New York on Friday, but if I stayed in San Francisco two more days and left Sunday morning, the round-trip fare would be only $450. I smelled a great consumer rip-off story and immediately called a major airline public relations officer to satisfy my curiosity and ask journalism's most important question: "Why?" I told him I was rolling tape. I planned to broadcast this exposé to the world.

"How can you charge so much more during the week," I asked indignantly, "when mostly business people are traveling? Are you not ripping off businesses?" I sat smugly back, waiting for my scoop to unfold.

"On the contrary," the savvy airline spokesman answered calmly, "what we are doing is giving weekend family travelers a tremendous discount."

"Oh" was about all I could muster as I stopped the tape, thanked the man, and hoped he wouldn't be telling that story over dinner.

Still, that "big curiosity" got a lot of us going at a young age.

Tom Brokaw recalls: "From the time I was a child just learning to speak, my parents and friends said that I had this almost genetic inclination to talk about what I had seen that day and what was going on around me . . . and that I seemed to remember what was important. My mother wanted to be a journalist. She worked in the post office and, as I often said, was the best journalist in the family, because she heard about everything that was going on. Everybody came to the post office in those days and told her stories, and she would come home at night and repeat them."

Brokaw found early inspiration not only from his mother's storytelling but also from heroes of his youth, like Edward R. Murrow. He remembers his first real exposure to broadcasting: He was sixteen. It was the fall of 1956.

It was the reelection of Dwight Eisenhower, as well as senatorial and congressional elections. I had been working nights at the radio station after basketball practice, and the guys who worked there were very encouraging, so they said come on down on election night and help us out. So I went racing around town collecting votes from the precincts and calling them in. And I remember driving by the newspaper, where they had a big chalkboard and they were writing down returns. Remember, the paper didn't come out until the next day. I thought, radio is so much better. We just call them in and bang—it's on the air. And everybody gets it right off the bat, and everybody listens to the radio out there.

I was up til two in the morning or something and I had school the next day, but I didn't care, I had a great time. I've often thought about that. That was probably the beginning. I remember thinking, what a wonderful way to make a living. And then Huntley and Brinkley came on the air about the same time. We had a black-and-white television set—we lived out there on the prairie, away from the population centers, away from the big cities and the cultural capitals of the world. That was a window on the world for me that I had never anticipated you could have. I was a great student of all correspondents, remembered all their names, the work they had done. I thought, maybe someday I could do that and NBC would pay for me to travel the world. And wouldn't that be exciting. And friends of mine from those days remember me talking about . . . that's what I wanted to do.

Brokaw chose NBC in his early fantasies about his future because of role models like Huntley and Brinkley. I chose CBS because while I was growing up I heard that particular network at home constantly. But not all our heroes floated in on the airways.

"I can't tell you the age exactly, but I was quite young because my role model was Brenda Starr."[1] Lynn Sherr of ABC news didn't have many female role models to choose from when she was growing up.

> I talk about this in speeches all the time . . . it was wonderful to have Brenda Starr as a role model. She was gorgeous; she was adventurous; she always got her story and she always got her man. I would have liked better to have a flesh-and-blood role model. There were many female reporters, as you well know, in the days when we were growing up, but they didn't get any publicity and nobody knew about them. Nellie Bly[2] was the only one you sort of knew about, and she was always under the category of crazy lady who did weird things, rather than solid, fabulous journalist.

I was seeing more parallels with my own career and those of Cronkite, Brokaw, and, now, Sherr. There were these little indicators in our young lives.

"I always knew," says Sherr.

> I just loved, from the time I was a little kid, telling people something they didn't know and telling them the story first. . . . When I was in grammar school my parents gave me, as a present one year, a little printing set. I don't know if you had one of these. You literally took the rubber letters and stuck them in the thing, and I printed a family newspaper. I always worked on the school paper—always—and I just always knew what I was going to do. There really wasn't much question in my mind.

---

1 Brenda Starr: A fictional comic strip woman reporter.

2 Nellie Bly: pseudonym for Elizabeth Cochrane Seaman (1867–1922). A celebrated pioneer in enterprise journalism, Bly spent ten days in a mental hospital so she could do a story on mental patients. She took a well-publicized trip around the world in seventy-two days, to beat the fictional time in the Jules Verne novel *Around the World in Eighty Days*. She wrote books in addition to working as a reporter for such papers as the *New York World*, the *New York Journal*, and the *Pittsburgh Dispatch*.

No question! *I* had no question. Dan Rather had no question. "It starts with a dream. I had my dream early, very early. I am not able to explain why, from the earliest time I can remember, when asked what I wanted to be, I always answered, 'I want to be a reporter.'"

Brian Williams, whose hero was Walter Cronkite, had no question in his mind either.

I knew what I wanted to do at about age five. The first recorded newscast I did was at age six. I published a newspaper about our family at age seven. Mine was always the first hand to shoot up in Current Events class. I knew the complete bio of Melvin Laird[3] by the time I was in junior high. I ran into Everett Dirksen[4] in the bathroom when I was with my parents in Washington in 1972, and I was able to carry on a conversation with him about what was going on in his life.

COMMON THREADS

Passion, Dan Rather confides, is a must for a climb to the top rung of journalism. "Journalism, as much or more than any craft or profession I know, requires passion. It requires *com*passion also, but it does require passion—a passion for the work." Not so, Rather points out, with respect to many other career undertakings. If it's journalism you're looking toward, you'd better have that passion. And a passion for information. It's one of those common threads we found.

BRIAN WILLIAMS: My father would casually bring home from work each day *Women's Wear Daily*, several newspapers, the *Wall Street Journal*, but chiefly the *New York Times*. And I made a vow at age fourteen, that I would never end a day without reading the *New York Times*. I've had vacations, I've had twelve-day trips to Asia, and I've never broken my vow. I've read every goddamn *Times*.

3 Melvin Laird: U.S. congressman (1952–1969), secretary of defense (1969–1973) under President Richard Nixon.
4 Everett Dirksen: U.S. congressman (1933–1949), U.S. senator (1951–1969), Senate Republican minority leader (1959–69).

DAN RATHER: It began way back in the midst of my childhood, dreaming of being a reporter. I have never known exactly why that was the case. I have come to believe it had something to do—maybe a lot to do—with the fact that my father was a voracious reader of newspapers. My mother was also an extremely avid reader. But my father just consumed newspapers. And he considered newspapers to be a poor man's university—and looking back on it, I think that probably has a great deal to do with it.

Common threads have a way of insinuating themselves in all sorts of places. I was asked to address a conference of school superintendents in New York State one spring. They wanted me to bring them a nice positive message about how great schools were doing in the lower Hudson Valley and the suburbs of New York. I couldn't do it. What I did do was recall my own formative years in public schools in New York City.

Back in the fourth grade, we each were required to bring in twenty-five cents every week to purchase five days' worth of newspapers. We had a choice between the *New York Times* and the *Herald Tribune*. I chose the *Trib*. We then spent forty-five minutes each day with our newspapers. We were to read through them, pick out an article that interested us, study it, and then stand before the class and report to them what we had learned from our chosen article. We were all becoming reporters. In the fourth grade! Nine years old! We were learning about current events, the neighborhood, the city, and the world. That's what got *me* interested in journalism.

Well, I told that to the superintendents. Do they do that in schools now? No! Did they have any intentions of doing so? No! Does it matter? Yes! But to do it today would probably be politically incorrect. Some kids wouldn't be able to afford the papers. The teachers would have to read the papers too, and that creates extra workload. It would take time. It would create stacks of newspapers that would then have to be recycled. Obviously, it is a bad idea.

IT'S NOT AS EASY AS IT LOOKS

Andy Rooney says one of the best things he has ever heard about journalism was said by an athlete, about another athlete. "Somebody was talking about Joe DiMaggio and they said, 'He never made a tough catch in his life.' That's great!" Rooney, considered one of the most creative writers on television, likewise makes it look easy. We all watch his Sunday night commentaries on *60 Minutes*—in which, by the way, he swears he never, ever said, "Did you ever wonder . . ."

Rooney never expected to wind up face to face with millions of Americans every week, talking about everyday things like how come no gloves are ever kept in a car's glove compartment. He always wanted to be a writer, and that's a side of him he wishes were more recognized.

You know, I wrote for a lot of other people before I wrote for myself. Harry Reasoner, Garry Moore, Arthur Godfrey. And then I did a lot of comedy for Sam Levinson and a lot of other people.

The make-it-look-easy part?

You hear what they're saying, and you get to be able to imitate their style. Just as someone who's good with his or her voice can imitate a voice, a writer who has an ear can imitate a writing style. I did find, and this was always interesting to me, that it was easiest for me to write for somebody who didn't really need me. Harry Reasoner was a very good writer. He was sort of lazy and didn't want to do it himself, and I could do it for him because he was very good himself. There are other people in the industry that I have tried to write for who can't write their own name, and I found it difficult to write for them.

Rooney had no problem writing prose that others got credit for.

No, I never minded that. I never intended to be on camera myself; it never interested me. I have a low opinion of actors, and I am nervous about having become somewhat, at least, an actor. The best work I ever did was before I got on television, and it irritates me that people don't know that. They think I'm just this *60 Minutes* person doing the three-minute pieces, but I never had any desire to be on camera. And if ten people knew that I wrote an hour-long documentary for Harry Reasoner, it was enough. My credit was up there. People in the industry knew I was the writer and the producer, and that was all I asked for. How much credit do you want? . . . I don't look at the ratings or anything, but if I meet somebody in the elevator and they say, "Hey, that was a nice piece you did last night," that's all I need. I like it. It's very nice. I'm not looking for the whole world to write me a letter.

Can we forgive Andy Rooney for calling Harry Reasoner "lazy"? You bet, and here's why. Rooney says he sometimes wonders about his own achievements.

I don't know how I did it. I mean for a basically lazy guy. I'll do anything to avoid going upstairs twice. I'll carry more than I can handle so that I only have to go upstairs once. My mother always said that was a lazy man's load, and it was. Yet, on the other hand, even being sort of lazy about a lot of things, I have incredible ambition. I suppose it's part ego, but I get up every morning at 5:25. I mean, I don't have any trouble. I am not only not bothered by that; I am anxious to get up and get to work. I enjoy it. I look forward to it. And this is some strange ambition. I am surprised I have as much of it as I have . . . and I think it's necessary to have it.

Lynn Sherr's ambition led her down a career path whose reality wasn't even close to her "Brenda Starr" fantasy.

I don't think I had a clue as to how much, shall we say, scut work, there is, and how much there is to do before you get to the good stuff: the good stuff being the actual reporting and then—tah-dum!—the actual either writing or producing or putting it on the air or putting it in print. There's a lot of stuff you have to do. This whole business of maintaining contact with people, working a source, keeping your phone lists up to date, being there at the right time. Half of it is luck, as you well know. Half of it is pure chance. You're there when something happens. But I think a certain amount of that comes from just having the instinct to be in the right place at the right time. I didn't know that there was a lot of that. But you know, I love the reporting part. I love the research part as well. So that has become part of the job.

A tolerance for scut work is not the only symptom of journalism fever. Mike Wallace notes that one can also be stricken with obsessive behavior.

> I suppose a great deal of it has to do with your motivation for get-ting into journalism in the first place. If you're just looking for a job, fine. If you're just looking to make some money, fine . . . it's perfectly straightforward and honorable and there's nothing wrong with it. But if you are stimulated by the chase, if you are stimulated by the process of digging, if you want to get behind the facade, then it becomes a lot more than just a nine-to-five job: It becomes a calling. It becomes almost an obsession. To find out how things work. To find out what goes on behind the scenes. To find out what motivates people.

All of which, Wallace adds, leads to the not-so-easy part:

> You have to have fresh eyes, you have to have curiosity, you have to have the willingness to work, to rise early and work late, to forget about your holidays, to be willing to get hooked on the job. And if you have that, the rewards, the satisfaction, the payback, are immense.

THERE IS NO FREE LUNCH

For all that payback, though, there is a giveback. In addition to mal-adies like obsession and workaholism, broadcast journalism can be haz-ardous to your physical health. Vernon Stone, professor emeritus at the University of Missouri School of Journalism, has been chronicling broad-cast journalism and journalists for many years. His latest report, support-ed by the Freedom Forum, is on the health-related problems of people in the television news business. Almost two thousand TV news people were surveyed. Bottom line: A third of those surveyed suffered stress-related problems, with symptoms like anxiety, headaches, fatigue, ulcers, heart trouble, and drug and alcohol abuse. The problems were evident across the gamut of jobs: from management, producers, and assignment editors to news photographers and reporters and even those "cushy" anchor jobs. In fact, two out of every five female anchors (and one out of every five male anchors) suffer from job-related stress. The report concludes that if the goal is less stress, one should aspire to do sports or weather.

It seems that the biggest cause of stress, in general, is loss of control over one's *time*. Anecdotal reports cite a great deal of family and marital stress growing out of the long hours of the news business (and the obsessive nature of journalists)—and long hours are an inescapable part of the news business. From calls I got at three in the morning rushing me to some fire to the police bulletin about an explosion that came in when I had one foot out the door at the end of a twelve-hour day, as a reporter I had no control over my own time. In fact, I *had* little of my own time. Even weekends and days off were spent working the phones or thinking about how to finish up an investigative piece in the works; it seemed I could never switch off my "journalist" mind. Lunch with a friend or colleague? Impossible to plan. More likely I would wind up eating a "tube steak" al fresco from the corner hot dog-and-ptomaine vendor while rushing to my car to get to yet another breaking event. A cigarette washed down with cold coffee often kept me going long into the dark, damp night as I waited with a covey of reporters for the punch line to the story we were covering.

For me, the short-term rewards for enduring that stress were indescribable adrenaline rushes. The long-term effects of that stress were one divorce; children I'm just getting to know now; two quadruple bypass surgeries, the first at age 43; a minor stroke; and a bad back from hauling equipment around all those years. Despite all of that, I can still say I loved it. No regrets? Actually, no *choice*. As I have often said, journalism chose me. I didn't choose it.

Money's Not the Motivator

One day, as Saint Peter was interviewing people before he let them enter heaven, he was talking to one fellow and asked how much money he made last year. The man replied, "Two hundred and fifty thousand dollars." Saint Peter responded, "Very nice, and what did you do?" "I was a lawyer" was his reply. As Saint Peter spoke to the next person in line, he asked the same questions. "I made three hundred and seventy-five thousand dollars last year," the woman said, "and I was a doctor." When Saint Peter asked the next person in line how much he had made, his response was, "Seventeen thousand two hundred dollars." To that Saint Peter said, "And what were your call letters?"

No joke. The average pay in radio and television is quite low—though the paycheck can be immense if you reach the heights of the industry. Still, money was not the motivating force for any of the cream of the crop when they went into it. Mike Wallace's drive to be in radio had nothing to do with economics; since college, he'd just been in love with the idea. Just out of college, persistence finally landed him a job at WOOD in Grand Rapids, Michigan. "I got the job—twenty bucks a week. And as soon as I started, I knew: This was what I had, unwittingly, dreamed of. This was the job that I wanted to do. I didn't have any desire to do anything else." His next job brought him up to fifty bucks a week.

Andy Rooney is an advanced amateur woodworker who takes great pride in the skills he has developed; he doesn't make his own furniture to save money. Let Rooney make the connection.

> Listen, you see a carpenter planing a board, and if you think he's just making a living, you're wrong. That carpenter is very interested in what that board is going to look like and how he's doing it, and he likes what he's doing. He's getting a great deal of satisfaction from those little shavings. He's making that board look nicer. And money, at that point, does not enter into his head. And that is absolutely the same with me and, I think, particularly with those of us in television news. I don't know anyone who wouldn't work for a tenth of what he's receiving.

Piles of cash did not float through Rooney's career dreams. "No, money had nothing to do with it. I'm working on a piece now about doctors. Doctors—they don't get into medicine for the money. Not most of them—not 90 percent of them."

There is, of course, plenty of money to be made, but most of it is made by a handful of journalists, far outnumbered by local reporters and news writers who toil for under twenty thousand dollars a year, with no overtime. They do it because they must.

"I think a lot of this is feeling driven," remarks Brian Williams. "You have to love this." Williams loved it enough to keep plugging along after being repeatedly turned down for on-air jobs as he searched for the fulfillment of his obsession. Did he ever come close to giving up the dream?

"Yeah, at moments when I've been told that I had failed. I couldn't get my tape seen by anyone. I couldn't imagine working outside of a newsroom, so I got a job typing Chyron[5] on the screen." Williams couldn't get on the air, but the gnawing need to be in the news business wouldn't subside.

I couldn't imagine going to work for a bank after having been in television. Even though everyone said, by their actions, that I was lousy, that I wasn't good enough to advance. That wasn't going to deter me—I don't scare easily. I still had a right to be near news. There were still plenty of other jobs that put me in a newsroom. I didn't have to be the top dog; I didn't have to be on camera. That should also be part of it—that you just *love* this. If I'm disfigured, God forbid, in an accident tomorrow, I'm still going to want to work in the news business. I won't be able to appear on the air anymore, but I'll write for somebody else to say it. I'll write for a newspaper. I'll do radio.

The adrenaline kick gets 'em every time. Williams defines it perfectly.

If your pulse doesn't increase appreciably, measurably, when you walk into a newsroom, get out. Honest to God, there is a physiological reaction I have, and other people who love the business have, walking into a newsroom. I was just out in Topeka at the NBC station there. I loved their newsroom. It's a newsroom. It's small; people are working hard for no money. It's just like the one in Pittsburgh, Kansas, which was a converted garage with the news vehicles out back, where I started. I was in Elmira, New York. Great newsroom: four desks pushed together in the middle of a room. Terrific—I don't care how small it is. Real news was being gathered and written.

You won't get an argument on that from any of us who've been through it. "Oh yes, he's absolutely right," notes Mike Wallace.

When I walk across the street and I walk into that newsroom, to this day, when I walk into the Rather news area, there's a kind of

5 Chyron: a method used to superimpose writing over the pictures on a television screen.

energy that's like . . . it's like walking into a . . . not a holy place, but it's the big time. It's adrenaline when you walk in there, and you see all these people looking at the wires and looking at the videos and talking over the news and writing stuff and so forth. It's just fascinating.

It's more than fascinating—it's *captivating*. I remember the sounds of newswire machines clacking away. There is a certain smell to electronics and an unmistakable smell to a news story about to break.

Don Hewitt, creator of *60 Minutes*, is renowned for his television achievements. When he last signed another five-year contract with CBS, Hewitt was 77 years old, and he said he'd sign another five-year deal when this one expired. Why? Because this is what he *has* to do. "I sometimes think I'm kind of an idiot savant." (He laughs.) "I do what I do very well, but I don't know that I would do anything else very well. I'm not sure I would be this big a success in print."

Print or television, it's storytelling—and that was Don Hewitt's dream.

Oh, yeah. When other kids were playing cops and robbers and cowboys and Indians, I was playing reporter. I don't know why, but I just . . . when I was a little kid, I just knew. I couldn't wait to get my first trench coat, smoke a pipe, and look like Joel McCrea in *Foreign Correspondent*.

I used to go to the movies every Saturday, and I had two heroes. There was a guy named Julian Marsh, who was the producer of *Forty-second Street*, and there was Hildy Johnson, the reporter in *The Front Page*. I never knew which one of those two guys I wanted to be. And the first time I walked into a television studio, I saw the lights and the cameras and the booms and the stagehands, and I also saw, over in the corner, there were eighteen newswire printers clacking away like crazy, and I said, "Holy shit! In television, you can be *both* those guys!" And it sort of happened.

"You never wanted to do anything else?"
"No, never! It's all I ever wanted to be."
The really excellent ones don't choose this business. It chooses them.

2

"It": What Ya Gotta Have

Every year, thousands of youngsters pick up a violin for the first time and screech out their very first notes. It's usually part of some elementary school music program, or it's because some older sibling or parent once played the violin. Some of these youngsters are suddenly filled with enthusiasm, practice hard, take advanced lessons, and discover that music is their passion. They will spend their lives playing the violin professionally. Many will go on to perform with symphony orchestras, string quartets, or Broadway theater orchestras and in recording studios. Some will appear as soloists, perhaps at Lincoln Center or even Carnegie Hall.

Yet, with all those violinists out there and more coming along every year, there is only one Isaac Stern . . . only one Jascha Heifitz . . . only one Itzhak Perlman. There's a reason for that. The truth is, whether you are a musician or a journalist, what it takes to excel is passion, but passion is not enough. To *really* excel, you have got to have "It." Here's how NBC's Brian Williams defines "It":

> I tell the story of traveling around the country with Clinton or just on business and checking into a hotel. The first thing I do, I have dinner downstairs, 'cause I'm a married man and I'm bored and I love to

read, and I go back to my room and I turn on the local ten or eleven o'clock news. I can tell you in the first thirty seconds who's going to make it out of that market. There is an "It." There is an "It," and it's both tangible and intangible. Students ask me all the time, "Well, am I doing the right things?" I had a student call me last week from George Washington University. "I'm in the School of Foreign Service. Will that look good on my resume?" And sadly, at the end of the day, if you don't have "It," it probably won't matter what your resume has on it.

"It" is a natural curiosity; "It" is a love for facts; "It" is a love for the news business, for newsgathering; and "It" is the ability to sit in front of a microphone or look into a camera and impart what you know, impart what you've learned. The night a plane crashes, that camera isn't going to turn off for about six hours. You had better damn well be on top of your game.

Or maybe it's something else. Brian Willliams continues, this time turning the tables:

> Art, you, for instance, were born gifted with a quirky set of pipes that made you sound different and authoritative and distinctive. I know an Art Athens piece playing on a radio from three miles away. And veteran New Yorkers were drawn to your work. We all knew we were going to get the story from you, of course, but something was going to make us do what I call a cocker spaniel: cock your head a little when you're listening, with an air of, "Hmmm, I hadn't thought of that."

Williams's ability to quickly know if someone has "It" is not unusual for those of us in the business. Casting directors can tell a tenor "Thank you for coming" before he gets to the second line of a song. When I was the news director at WABC Radio in New York, I received dozens of unsolicited audition tapes every week. I could tell in twenty seconds whether to listen further to a sample newscast or story.

I know, I know. What about all this talk about substance, about good writing? Aren't *they* what's important? Yes, they are. But first, you, the listener, have to hear that certain something. *Then* you listen for the writing and the substance. If the "It" isn't there, the rest will hardly matter. And if it is? Well, here's a case in point from Andy Rooney:

> I think it's very difficult to define excellence. Why is Walter Cronkite the best anchorman there ever was? I suppose you could sit down and figure it out. He's bright, he's inquisitive, he cares about the world; but there is some indefinable quality he has that would be very difficult to put down in words. I don't know what it is.

Not only does Rooney have trouble defining it; so does Walter Cronkite.

> I have no idea. The only thing I can think of is my own personal, inner intensity to try to get it right and to communicate it. I never had any sense of the cosmetics of being on the air. I never really thought of how I looked or how I sounded. As a matter of fact, I was so uninterested I probably made a mistake: I never looked at tapes. I never looked at a broadcast I did unless somebody else wanted to look at it and I had to sit through it. But anything that was on tape, I avoided as much as I could.

People like Dean Daniels, a former executive producer and news director for WCBS-TV in New York, always looked for "It" in the people they hired.

> I looked for a couple of things, because of the medium I was in. Obviously, the way people looked. That's not to say whether they were pretty; when I say the way people looked, I mean how they visually presented themselves and carried themselves on camera. That was a big part of it, because that was part of the communication "set." You could be a great writer and be haltingly distracting in your delivery on air. And it didn't matter how good the writing was, unfortunately, because it is a visual medium and people make judgments, and I didn't think anybody would ever be able to get past it.

"However," I commented to Daniels, "all that is gold does not always glitter. Charles Kuralt, for example, was probably one of the best communicators in the world. And," I pointed out, "Kuralt was a fat, bald guy."

"And his writing style," added Daniels, "was unparalleled."

His writing style was wonderful because he made you see pictures. He made you *feel* things. But his *delivery* is what sold it. His delivery was so perfect, it was almost like listening to a well-composed song being sung by Louis Armstrong, who had a terrible voice. "He was a great *communicator*," observes Daniels.

> I always looked for people who were believable, who could tell good stories, who could be parachuted into a situation and do the appropriate thing—and every situation has different appropriate things to do. You didn't have to be the best reporter in the world to necessarily work in one of my shops. But you had to be able to tell good stories.

As we've seen, those who have "It" may not be aware that they have it, or exactly what it is they do have. They know it's something, but they're not sure what. Two of the best communicators in broadcasting are Charles Osgood and Andy Rooney. Surely they have "It." But Andy isn't sure what it is he has. He takes a guess for us.

> Well, I have an outstanding averageness about myself. I am quintessentially average. I think people sense that I am no more of an intellect and no more intellectual than they are, and not any smarter than they are. I have recognized the universality of a lot of little ideas more than they have, but other than that, they think of me as themselves.

Brian Williams wonders about the likes of Osgood, considered one of the best writers in broadcasting.

> Essayists like Osgood are just nothing short of brilliant. They are an absolute pleasure to listen to, but why are all the other essayists so bland? What makes people connect with a certain personality? I don't know. I suppose you and I would have one hell of a consulting business if we knew.

What does Osgood himself think he has?

One of the things that I had no idea I could do when I first got into radio was write; I'd never written anything but a letter. It astounds me that this is my reputation, because I hadn't the first idea how to do it. I think I was a pretty quick learner at that time. Once given the opportunity to do it, I think I discovered myself.

Osgood, too, pursued the elusive secret of what "It" might be, and he had a role model.

There was one point when I started working at CBS that I really seriously considered going into the front office and saying, "Would you be willing to let me just hang out with Charles Kuralt and see how he does it? All I know is, that when he does a piece, it's full of wonder. I mean, marvelous things happen on the screen. He has a sense that he communicates to you: a warmth, a humanity—but I don't know how he does it. If I could just see how or where he gets it or the steps that get him to the point where he does what he's aiming to do." I never worked up the courage to do that, but I told him about it. He just sort of laughed.

Ironically, when Kuralt left CBS shortly before he died, Charles Osgood took over Kuralt's coveted role as host of *CBS News Sunday Morning.*

Would Kuralt have been able to teach Osgood what the "It" factor was? Probably not. Kuralt told me one day:

I'm not really very introspective, and I haven't really thought about these things very much. I have a feeling that I wouldn't be a very good teacher, because I could tell a class everything I know in an hour, and then what do you do the second hour? I asked that question of the dean of the School of Journalism in Chapel Hill and he said, "The second hour you assign papers."

It would be very hard—I mean, especially if somebody said, "OK, there are forty students sitting in this classroom. I want you to go in there and tell them how to do it." Well, I couldn't . . . I would have no idea what to do. People have suggested to me that I might like to teach when I get out of this, but I have no idea how to teach anybody.

Perhaps that's because there really isn't any way to teach "It." Charles Osgood points out that the quest to define "It" is age-old.

There's a scene in the movie *Amadeus* that reminds me—see if it reminds you—of what we have just been talking about. Salieri waits out in front of Mozart's house until he sees Mozart leave, so he knows there's nobody in there but the housekeeper. And he goes to the front door and the housekeeper tells him, "Mr. Mozart's not here. He just left." "Such a pity," Salieri says. "It's very important that I . . . may I wait for him?" "Of course." You didn't say no to this guy; he was a very important man. Salieri says, "You know, in fact, let me wait in the music room." So they usher him into the place and he says, "I'll be fine. Just let me wait." So the housekeeper leaves. Salieri wanders around the room, thinking, "So this is the piano and this is the pen. So he sits here and the window's over there and he . . ." He's trying to figure out . . . how does Mozart do it? He's trying to figure out how in the hell he does it. And he's looking at the physical surroundings.

It's like someone asking me, "How do you write? On a PC or a laptop? Do you write with a pen or a pencil, or with a typewriter? How do you do it? Is there some secret I can learn by looking at the mechanics of what you do?" And the answer, of course, is no.

THE LITMUS TEST

Have you ever been to an event—perhaps a wedding or anniversary—where someone, usually a relative, gets up to sing a song with the band? They are so God-awful, you wonder how they themselves don't realize how bad they really are. You wonder what possessed them to even consider getting up in front of a bunch of people and performing. Well, news executives get audition tapes like that all the time. We listen to, watch, or read the stuff and think the aspiring journalist should really be looking into the insurance business. Not that there's anything wrong with insurance.

If that singer could hear what she really sounds like, would she be up in front of that band? Probably not. Same for the audition tape. That's why I asked Dan Rather and others to come up with a "litmus test."

I wanted something that could be self-administered: questions one should ask oneself before venturing into the real world. Before getting up in front of the band, so to speak. I figured it would save them, and the rest of us, a lot of grief. Rather came up with these "questions to ask yourself if you're considering committing yourself to a career in journalism":

1. Do you love the news? It's the absolute base requirement: You have to love the news.
2. Do you burn with a hot, hard flame to do this? I don't think it's required in some other fields, but in journalism, you have to burn constantly with an inextinguishable hot, hard flame to do it. I used to say to myself, "I can't do anything else with my life. I have to find a way to make a living at this, because I can't do anything else."
3. Do you like to write? Do you either write well already, or do you want to learn to write well enough to really dedicate yourself to writing? Writing is the fundamental bedrock skill of the craft, whether you're going to be in print, on radio, on television, or on the Internet.

My point here is, one should not kid oneself. Suppose your honest assessment of yourself is that you *don't* write and/or you don't like to write—or at the very least, you don't think that you can pour yourself into a lifetime of making yourself at least an adequate writer. Then I would see that as a very large cautionary flag about not getting into the craft—'cause you might be headed for heartbreak.

Certainly there are people who did not meet this standard who have "made it." Some of them have made it big. But things are changing, and I'm a look-ahead person. As far ahead as I can look, I'll stand by my feeling that one of the tests you can give yourself is, "How do I feel about writing?"

Andy Rooney adds to that list a belief system check.

If you believe that an informed electorate is the best hope for the democratic system and that the democratic system is the best hope for happiness for the most people, then informing—being part of the system that informs the electorate, to enable them to make wiser choices—is a highly honorable and elevated calling.

While not many journalists may ever even have thought of that, or thought to put it down on paper or even say it, this is the motivating force—trying to present the most number of people with the truth. I mean, if all the truths were known about everything by everyone, it would be a better world. And this is the journalist's motivating force. He believes that.

Tom Brokaw also has a couple of questions budding journalists should ask themselves. And Brokaw's contribution adds insight into what today's successful journalist can look forward to.

I think you have to ask yourself whether you're prepared to be brave. I don't mean physically brave, but intellectually brave. You have to be willing to go against conventional wisdom in the search for facts. And you should be willing to tilt against windmills in the Don Quixote sense. You should be willing to not have a conventional life, because journalism can be uncomfortable, both for the readers and viewers and for those people who are in the profession. You've got to ask uncomfortable questions. You've got to make people think about things that they would rather not think about sometimes. You have to have intellectual and moral integrity if you want to be a journalist.

In case that doesn't sound complex and stressful enough, I asked Brian Williams about those times when it's two in the morning, you're exhausted, you're doggedly chasing another fact, and your spouse yells to you to "go to bed already."

Yeah. That's hard, too . . . that can't be taught. I think it's safe to say that 90 percent of the time, the people who can't put it down—those will be the best journalists. A good story is like a good book; you're never quite finished with it. It lives with you for a long time. You know, if you don't have natural curiosity, you're not finished in this business, but you're not going to do as good a job as the person next to you who does.

Now, let's go back to that relative singing with the band while everyone in the room cringes. Similar cringing can go on in a newsroom when the wrong person gets a foot in the door. Just ask Lynn Sherr.

> You know, I have this conversation with people, and I have it in my head. When I see someone who's not trained or instinctively a journalist who gets brought into our business—these so-called pretty faces, male or female—I always wonder, "Is it possible. Can you learn it?" I think the answer is . . . you cannot learn the basics of journalism.
>
> You can learn the skills; you can learn how to write; you can learn how to put a story together—sort of—but you cannot learn the curiosity, you cannot learn the energy and the drive, and you cannot learn the instinct for wanting to tell the truth. And that to me is terribly important, and I'm not going to name any names, but you know who they are as well as I do. A bunch of people out there, particularly in my business, still don't have the right instinct for asking questions. When they interview someone they're asking about themselves, or they're asking off to this side or off to that side. They don't understand how you ask a question. And I don't think you can understand that if you don't have it in you. You can learn a certain amount, but you can't learn it all.

If you don't know how to dance and have no rhythm, you should probably stay off the dance floor. If you don't know much about news, about what's going on in the world, you should probably stay off the air. Yet every night we see people on the air who shouldn't be there, because they obviously have no idea what they're talking about. They don't understand the story they are covering and they think they can fake it—but they can't. Brian Williams says he sees them so often he's tempted to make notes and write his own book.

> I saw a piece on CNN the other night from some reporter on a Miami affiliate that enraged me almost to the point of calling the news director at the station and saying, "What were you thinking? What are you doing? Get that woman off the air." No one was being served by her covering a story. She was so God-awful, even the imparting of

the facts was hampered by her delivery—by her clear lack of under-standing of what's going on.

CHOICES

It boils down to choices. People have to decide if they have what it takes to be journalists. Managers have to decide whom to hire and put on the air. Viewers have to decide whether the chosen ones are worth watching. And individual journalists have to decide if they want to just be on the air or if they want to excel. When an excellent manager connects with an excellent broadcaster, magic can happen, for them and for us.

Mike Wallace points out that there is always that chance.

If you care about it, you'll go to the smallest market. I find it impossible to believe that almost anybody doesn't have a chance to make it in radio and/or television, if you care enough about it. You don't have to be the best-looking person in the world. You don't have to have the best voice in the world. You don't have to be the best writer in the world. But if you *care* enough, that will communicate itself, first of all to your potential bosses and eventually to the audi-ence—in radio and in television. Beyond a shadow of a doubt.

The trick is to identify the "It" factor, which, Brian Williams and I agree, is not so easy.

Let's be honest. You and I have both achieved something everyone working at the local media level wants to do, and that is we have worked in the number one media market—love it or hate it—in the United States. That is New York. And for the foreseeable future, it will *be* New York. So you can make a pretty sweeping assumption about us: that someone decided we had "It." "It" is very hard to come by. "It" jumps off the screen at you, it jumps off the page at you. Love 'em or hate 'em, there are op-ed writers with "It." They have, maybe it's a flair for the dramatic. Maybe [*New York Times* columnists] Maureen Dowd and Frank Rich know how to reach out and grab the jugular, while another columnist seems like an old, worn-out song.

Dowd and Rich may enrage, while another may bore people. Maybe that's the difference.

As a Supreme Court justice once said of pornography, "I know it when I see it." So do we all recognize "It" when it appears?

"Today is the funeral of the widow of Malcolm Ten."

PHILADELPHIA NEWS ANCHOR ON THE DEATH
OF THE WIDOW OF MALCOLM X

3

HANKERING TO BE ANCHORING
—I WANNA BE A STAR—

It is estimated that two out of three young journalism hopefuls, upon entering broadcast journalism school, want to come out the other end as anchors. And why not? They grew up seeing news anchors—both local and network—marketed and touted as TV stars. They've read about the multimillion-dollar deals. They know that anchors make the most money, get the most "face time," and become the most well known. And they don't have to stand out in the heat or the rain or the cold of winter to cover a story. They can work on their smile and their hair in an air-conditioned studio and just "throw it" to the poor reporter who is standing knee-deep in a snowdrift.

Many of these hopeful young anchors change their minds once they get down to the business of learning the process. They turn to producing, writing, photography, editing, or reporting. Some even decide on print.

The truth is, believe it or not, many who are now anchors would rather be out there in the snow. They often cast a longing eye at the assignment board. For example, when a hurricane hits, you'll generally find Dan Rather, soaking wet, hair askew, standing in the thick of it trying to talk over a howling wind, for tens of hours on end to get the story— and he *loves* it.

Same thing for Tom Brokaw. In fact, in a sense, Brokaw was tied to the anchor desk kicking and screaming all the way.

Look, Art, there was a time in my life—a lot of times in my life—when I could've just settled for being a local news reader. I had the skills; every program I ever did was successful in the ratings; and there were lots of times when they were trying just to have me be the local anchor. I never wanted to do that. You know, they had to drag me into the studio every time—and I would spend more time in the studio than I wanted to. I only wanted to be a reporter. I only wanted to be out there.

When I was in California as a local anchor as well as a network correspondent, I worked effectively a double shift. I worked by day as a correspondent and then did the eleven o'clock news, because the network said, "That's where we're going to make the money, and *you're* going to make money, too." I finally said, "I can't do this anymore. I want to be just a correspondent." When I was at the White House, at the end of two years of Watergate, they came and said, "We want you to do the *Today* show—but you have to do commercials." I said, "I'm not going to do that. I just won't do that." And a year later they said, "You don't have to do the commercials, but you have to do *Today*." I said, "OK . . . Yeah. I'll go try that for a while."

Then, at the end of five years of that I said, "I want to go back to being a reporter again." They said, "Well, you have to be the *Nightly News* anchor with Roger [Mudd], but you get to do more reporting." And the three of us—Dan [Rather], Peter [Jennings], and I—we've been reporters as much as we've been anchors. Peter just got back from India. I've been out in Milwaukee shooting a big documentary. You know, what we live for is not 6:30 at night putting on makeup and reading out loud. It's just a lot more rewarding, it's a lot more fun, turning over rocks and finding out what's going on.

Lynn Sherr is certainly an active "rock turner." Did she ever hanker to be an anchor?

The possibility didn't exist for me when I was a kid, so it wasn't what I wanted to be. I enjoy anchoring from time to time, as long as I can also report. I have never wanted to be just the face in the studio. I like it when I *do* it. I've filled in for every anchor job here at ABC, and it's fun. But it's much *more* fun to report. The values are skewed, so the pretty faces on the air get more money and more exposure than the people out in the field who are doing the work. It's a totally backward sense of values. But that's what management decided to do.

Just how much does management think an anchor is worth? Well, believe it or not, according to some industry surveys, small-market anchors (who probably constitute the bulk of the industry) can make as little as twelve thousand dollars a year. Big-market anchors (New York, Los Angeles) can make a couple of million. The average nationwide salary at the turn of this century was in the sixty thousand dollar range, with many middle-size-market anchors earning a healthy six figures.

There are great tales of anchors commanding and getting sweetheart deals and, more recently, of anchors losing those same deals. Just one specific case will serve as an example of what's happening industrywide.

News anchor Ann Martin has spent over twenty years of her life in the Los Angeles market, most of them at KABC-TV, which was number one in the Los Angeles news market. So along comes KCBS, which wasn't doing nearly as well, and they hire her away for a price tag of close to two million dollars a year. News consultant Don Fitzpatrick picks up the story.

> So she goes over to KCBS, and the feeling was that she had been in the market for so long, she'd been on the number one station for so long, that people—because they like her so much—would start watching KCBS and not watch KABC. Well, it just didn't happen that way. People were used to watching KABC, and they weren't used to watching KCBS. In many cases they didn't even know where she'd gone. They just knew that she wasn't on KABC anymore. And the person who replaced her did a credible job. So out of habit, they just stayed with KABC. So now KCBS is like five or six as far as ratings go.

To make a long story short, when Ann Martin's contract came up for renewal, she was offered about a 50 percent *cut* in pay. Now, when you're cut to only a million a year, most of us might say, "Gee, that's tough. Only a million a year . . . and who wants to be just a millionaire?" The reasoning behind the pay cut? Fitzpatrick speculates it's because she didn't deliver her KABC audience to KCBS as they had hoped. So they were ready to dump her for much cheaper talent. Actually for much, much, *much* cheaper talent. The figure we've been able to dig up (these things aren't discussed much in public) is a replacement anchor, already at the station, ready to sit in Ann Martin's chair for a measly quarter of a million dollars a year.

Ann Martin's agent, Ed Hookstratton,[1] says it was not Ann's fault the station's ratings were so low. He blames poor management at CBS—but not the management that originally hired Ann Martin.

> That management is gone. Another management came in, and then they were replaced by the Westinghouse group—and they were terrible. I mean, they have mismanaged everything they've ever touched in broadcasting. And he [CBS Stations Chief Jonathan Kline] decided, from a chair in New York or Philadelphia where he was sitting, "Why do we have to pay one and a half million to an anchor in LA? We're not winning out there." It's not her fault. The news wasn't any good—they were coming up short all the time. So they say, "Let's put the girl on that's making two twenty-five—put her on. What do we care? It's all the same—we're still going to get the same [ratings] number."

It was an attempt to dump Ann Martin without actually firing her. The station was all set with a press release announcing the new replacement anchor when, with fifteen minutes to go, a deal was struck. Ann Martin, according to her agent, got $1.2 million. How come? They ain't talkin', but very often an agent who represents such big network stars as Bryant Gumbel has enough clout to make deals for lesser clients. By the way, Ann Martin is still at KCBS as of this writing, and is reported to be very happy there. And KCBS is still reported to be doing, according to observers, "not very well." (No reflection on Ann Martin intended.)

---

1 Ed Hookstratton: Los Angeles–based lawyer/agent who represents about forty high-powered clients, including Bryant Gumbel and Tom Brokaw.

The news director at KCBS at the time all this went on was Larry Perett, who is now a broadcast news consultant. He left KCBS just before the final deal was closed. While Perett won't talk specifically about the Ann Martin case, he offers some perspective on what went on there, and what is still going on all over the industry.

When the [Ann Martin] deal came up, it was because of the situation within the company. That doesn't mean the television station, it means the CBS Television Network, the stations division. Basically, we had been seeking to get really large salaries down, and that was not new. That was not something that started with Ann. It was something that was going on routinely. It started out years ago in the 1980s in the top cities. What happened was that we managers, all of us, were faced with orders something like, "OK—You've got to cut two million out of your budget." So where do you go? You've got to go to the big-ticket items—and those are the salaries of the anchors, or the weather, or sports, or a highly paid reporter talent; but most of the time it's going to be anchors.

When we're faced with this we have no choice, because salaries make up most of our operating budget. So you have to go to those people. And you can't take union people down, because they're all being paid under union contracts. For example: I have a weather guy. He was making like four hundred thousand, and so we took him down to three hundred thousand. You know, stuff like that.

And is a highly paid anchor or weather or sports person likely to say, "You can *stuff* stuff like that?" Not likely. I don't know how many times over my career, during contract negotiations, I've heard these words from bosses in one form or another: "Do you know how many people there are out there who would take your job in a minute for half your pay?"

4

TELL ME A STORY
~WHAT EVERY REPORTER NEEDS TO DO, AND HOW TO DO IT~

The role of journalism in society today is still being hotly debated. Do you tell the public what it *needs* to know, or only what it *wants* to know? Fact is, it doesn't matter which side you agree with. A journalist tells a story. Nothing more; nothing less.

60 Minutes is the most popular news magazine show ever on television. Don Hewitt, its creator and long-time executive producer, says the popularity of the show is not an accident.

> The secret of *60 Minutes* is, you know, four words that every kid in the world knows: "Tell me a story." And I frequently go into a screening room and I say, "What's the story? Tell me the story." I love stories. Mike [Wallace] will write an opening and I don't know what he's talking about sometimes, and I say, "Mike, Mike, when you went home last night and Mary said to you, 'What's your story about this week?' and you said, 'Well, you know, there's this guy who lives in a house on a hill and he had trouble with his brother and one day they came to fisticuffs, and so on.' Tell the audience what you told Mary last night. Don't give me a lot of horseshit copy."
>
> Occasionally we get these blue sheets, which are an assignment for a story, and this is the story you want to tell: It's about a guy who did

this, and this, and this . . . And I say, "Yeah, it's a pretty good story. Let's tell it." But when I get to the screening room, I say, "Listen, I saw the blue sheet, but I don't recognize the story. Tell them what you told me when you sold me the idea." It's that simple.

Do You Qualify

How do you know whether or not you are a good storyteller? I recall an eighth-grade class in which we were all supposed to read a nonfiction book and then give an oral report to the entire class. Procrastinator that I was, the day for the oral reports came before I'd even considered what book I would read. Since my last name begins with the letter A, naturally I was called upon first.

Adrenaline raced through my body as I slowly rose to my feet and stepped to the front of the classroom. I then proceeded to make up an entire story—something about an African safari—though I actually knew very little about African safaris. The class and, more important, the teacher found the story enthralling. I got an A.

You might think I would have felt lucky and somewhat surprised by my good fortune, but as I look back on it now, I realize that when I stepped up to the front of that classroom, I never had a doubt that I would do well. I knew how to tell a story.

Some are obviously more skilled at storytelling than others. Linda Ellerbee, who has served as a reporter and anchor for both CBS and NBC, now produces and reports documentaries for her own company, Lucky Duck Productions. It was her ability to tell a story that brought her into journalism.

Many people in journalism feel that they were called to it. I've never felt that it's a calling. It is a *craft*, and it deserves our respect, but it's *not* a calling. I suppose in one sense I knew as a kid that I would be a storyteller in some fashion. I grew up among storytellers in Texas, but also—and I think this is important—I was a little girl. I was not given a lot of pictures of what girls could grow up and be. I did not want to be a nurse; I did not want to be a teacher; I did not want to be a mommy. What was left?

Well, one of the things left was a newspaperwoman. I had seen all those movies. I grew up in Texas, where a lot of people wanted to be

Lyndon Johnson and I, of course, wanted to be Hildy Johnson [a tough Chicago newspaperman in the classic Ben Hecht/Charles MacArthur play *The Front Page*; a woman in the 1940 Howard Hawks movie remake *His Girl Friday*].

Ellerbee says she worked on her college newspaper, but a year and a half into her studies she quit school, got married, had a baby, and wound up in Alaska, where, she says, her husband left her for a younger woman. Ellerbee was 28 and on her own.

I knew when my husband left me that I had to do something. And journalism was what occurred to me instantly. As a kid I had been there, but then I had gone on the girl-wife-mommy track. Also, the only thing I knew how to do was to tell a story. We like to call it storytelling, and a lot of people like to call it bullshitting . . . but it is an art. And it was an art in my family. If you didn't get things in the right order, if you tried to tell a story and you got your beginning and middle and end messed up, you never got to finish. So you learned early—in the hardest way possible—that if you wanted to get what you had to say out, you had to make a story out of it.

For me, news is not complicated. News is basically the answer to the question, "What happened?" We find out what happened, and then we tell people. People think it's just the finding out. No, no, no, no, no. If it were just the finding out, it'd be different. As we find out, then we tell people. This is why we're no good at keeping secrets. That's not what we do for a living. We tell stories.

MAKING THE RIGHT CHOICES

Assuming you are a storyteller, how do you know which story to tell? It has to be right for your audience, for your editor, and, most important, for yourself.

Arguably the best twentieth-century storyteller in the broadcast industry was Charles Kuralt. Not only did he know *how* to tell a story; he had a particular knack for choosing stories that perhaps no one else would have thought of as stories at all. That ability led to his long-running "On the Road" series on CBS and his long-time role as host of *CBS News Sunday*

Morning. Even after his death in 1997, Kuralt's writing is still revered, and his choice of subject matter still unmatched. Somehow, it seems, Kuralt could always find stories where there didn't seem to *be* any stories.

It's hard to characterize the "On the Road" stories. I didn't have a category or an idea. It's just, instinctively or from experience, I knew when I heard about one, that this was likely to turn out to be a pretty good story. And I was almost never wrong. Izzy Blackman, the cameraman, really helped me. He would see kids swinging from a rope tied to the limb of a tree and he'd say, "Oh gee, that's an awful pretty picture. If you could think of something to say about that, let's do it." And he was always encouraging me.

It takes time to develop the instincts to know a good story from a bad one. For Kuralt, it was an evolution.

The reason that I went to those feature stories, to tell you the honest truth, was that I didn't like the competitiveness and the deadline pressure and the opportunities for making an ass of yourself that existed in covering real news. When I started I was a newspaper reporter in Charlotte, North Carolina, my hometown. I had been editor of the college daily, which was the best job I ever had: You can just fill the page with your own opinions, and it's great. But when I really went to work on a paper, I found that I just hated—I mean my first job was calling the widow of some guy who had been shot to death the day before and getting a quote. I just hated that. I hated bothering her. You know, it was embarrassing. And so I guess I didn't really ever have the true reporter's instinct.

The first time I ever went to Vietnam for CBS, we were with the Vietnamese Rangers. This was before the U.S. was in the war with combat troops. We got ambushed, and these guys I had been friendly with for a couple of days were just lying dead all over the ground. The cameraman and I had the same instinct. We hated to take pictures of it, because it was embarrassing to those still alive that they had been defeated so badly. And, you know, most of the other reporters who covered Vietnam would have known they were on to a great story, all this shooting and then all this death, and I just hated it.

We shot it, but kind of discreetly and I just didn't like that kind of story. I don't think I was any more afraid than any other reporter would have been in that situation; it was just that I was embarrassed.

Kuralt picked his battle, not covering hard news, and he won. Others wound up on the street, covering so-called "hard" news stories the best they could. He would do a different kind of story.

Tom Brokaw on picking your storytelling fights:

It was not so long ago, in this very newsroom, the *Nightly News* newsroom, when toxic shock syndrome became known as a danger to women. There were men out there who controlled *Nightly News* who did not want the word "menstruation" on the air. They didn't want to talk about sanitary napkins on the air. Who needs to deal with that? Well, more than 50 percent of the American television audience is made up of women. It was a critical health issue for them. So this was one of the times that we said, "This is nuts. You've got to do this." And the women here who were still just researchers and clerks and so on said, "This is really important to us." And that has been a huge change.

Linda Ellerbee, on the same theme:

If you believe with all your heart that you're right, you really ought to fight with all your might to do it your way. But, having said that, everyone who has lasted in this business more than ten minutes knows you have to pick your battles. You can't go to the wall every time, because even in this age of five hundred networks, you will eventually run out of them. So it's important to pick and choose. I do believe, and I see this not happening very much today, I think it's important for each journalist to set boundaries for yourself, moral boundaries, and to try and stick to them.

A good example here is the "How do you feel about . . .?" The reporter gets to the scene, goes running up to the site of the plane crash, if you will, or the traffic accident or whatever, and what happens? She or he sticks a microphone in the face of the mother whose son has just died, who may still be lying there bleeding to death, and says, "How do you feel about your son lying there?" Now, to me that's the act of a moral dwarf. It is also, and I think even more crucially, real evidence of a lack of a better idea. It's just lazy reporting. There are many ways, both on radio and on television, that you can convey the sadness of that moment without intruding on the personal tragedy of someone standing there. So when young people come into the business and they say, "Well, if I don't ask that question, I'll be fired," my answer is, "Think your way out of it. What your news director is really telling you is he or she wants a good story, OK? So you figure out a way to tell a good story that meets your news director's needs and jibes with your personal feelings about what you don't want to do."

I can remember how I felt when, in the mid-1970s, I was struggling to get information about Eastern Airlines Flight 66; it had just crashed on its approach to Kennedy airport. I finally got through to an inside Eastern number. We knew nothing about the flight other than its number and that it had crashed just short of the JFK runway in New York. Where was it from? How many were on board? I asked an unsuspecting customer service rep, "What can you tell me about Flight 66?" The cheerful response was, "Flight 66 is on time and should be landing just about now, sir."

"Then you haven't heard?"

"Heard what, sir?"

My heart pounded as I realized what was happening, but I could do nothing but be direct. "Flight 66 just crashed at the end of your runway."

"Oh God! Oh God! Oh my God!" Her horrified outcry was cut off as she hung up.

Some months later, my editor asked me to make an early morning call to a family who lived in upstate New York. He told me to ask them how they felt about their son being killed during the night in a peacetime border dispute in Korea. "If you want to find out how they feel," I blurted out, "call them yourself!"

He didn't.

LOOK THE OTHER WAY

Sometimes, the obvious story isn't the story you really want at all—that is, if you want to make your own mark in the world. Sometimes the best story is where no one else is looking. CBS correspondent Charles

Osgood related a perfect example to me. It is an example of how a story-teller's view of a major event can be at least as memorable—perhaps even more memorable—than the event itself.

The date itself is memorable: November 22, 1963, the day President John F. Kennedy was assassinated. Osgood, who worked for ABC at the time, was having lunch with colleagues Stu Klein and then newcomer Ted Koppel at McGlade's, the popular network hangout less than a block from ABC's Manhattan studios.

All of a sudden there's this sort of buzz, and they turned up the radio and I hear, "shots fired at President Kennedy in Dallas today, blah, blah, blah," and we're sitting there. Ted and I wanted to get back, but they had to get us the check . . . and in the meantime, Stu Klein is gone. He's not there anymore. And we did the right thing, we stayed, we got the check, we paid for the check, we waited for the change. But by the time we got back Stu Klein is sitting in the studio at ABC, and he's on the air. Now we knew that he knew no more than we did [about what had happened in Dallas]. But he had gotten back to ABC, which was panicking; in fact, ABC ended up borrowing cash from McGlade's to send enough people to Dallas. Meanwhile, Stu had apparently started taking in information the second it happened. This thing that he was now doing on the air was a piece about a bar in Manhattan: people sitting at the bar, a man in overalls, somebody else wearing a hat, a woman carrying a bag of groceries, a guy . . . you know, he was still talking about the people who were there at the bar. Out on the street cars are pulling over to one side, doors are opening, people are gathering around cars listening to what's being said. And he had not gone half a block and he had captured something about that par-ticular moment just by looking—just by being observant.

What's the lesson in that?

The lesson is to keep your eyes open and to realize that just because your story isn't where everybody else is—just because nobody has done that particular story—doesn't mean that it's not a story that's worth doing. The fact is, as it turns out, I remember that story after all these years.

At the time, recalls Osgood, the public response to Stu Klein's story was immense. People immediately related to it, because it was about *them*. Remember, Klein had no script. He was literally telling a story, as he spoke.

> It was a written piece in a way. I mean, he'd gone back and made a lot of notes of all the different little things that he had seen, and it was done with a lot of detail; he didn't just make it up. He described a cab driver—a black cab driver who had pulled his car over and was holding his head, and somebody else who was crying, and somebody else who was . . . you know. It was just a marvelous piece of business that taught me so much about how the story is whatever you see, and just telling it is a thousand times better than typing it.

> Generally, if you're a storyteller, your gut instinct is the right instinct.

> Stu was a very experienced news guy. He knew what he was doing. He knew that he couldn't do a piece about what does this mean for the world, or for the country, or whatever; he didn't know enough about that. But he could talk about what a punch in the stomach it was to everybody.

WHAT THEY SEE IS WHAT YOU GET

Writers are always told to "write what you know." If you are going to write about people, you have to know about those people first. How they think. What they talk about. What they care about. How they behave. Instinct is also a major instrument in a reporter's toolbox. Longtime colleague Jerry Nachman was considered a newsman's newsman. He ran radio and television newsrooms in several major markets, including New York, Washington, D.C., and San Francisco. He did a stint as editor-in-chief of the *New York Post*. He was a columnist and a guest panelist and TV pundit on various network shows, generally where he could contribute some of his earthy perspective on the politics of a specific situation, or on politics in general. Before all of that, he was a Damon Runyonesque, hard-nosed street reporter on the toughest streets in the world: the sidewalks and alleys of New York City.

When it came to relying on your "gut" in telling a story, Nachman says, many a good storyteller honed that gut at the bar rail of the local watering hole, in neighborhoods where the stories were being played out. "Reporters, to me, were the Danny Meenans[1] of the world. The Pete Hamills.[2] Some were elegant, like Hamill; some were inelegant, like Danny; but they would go to a bar and put their feet up on a rail. They'd talk to a dockworker and smell what that guy's world was like."

It is not unusual for a reporter to be assigned to a story he or she knows nothing about. A good reporter is a quick study, an aggressive listener, and a keen observer. While even the reporter may soon consider him- or herself to be an "instant expert" on a subject, the truth is that a good reporter becomes a vessel for information well received and analyzed. As Nachman often noted to his news staff, a reporter's goal is always to find out what is going on. Search for the truth. "And they *did* care about the truth. When we started, we didn't have an agenda about who was right and who was wrong. There was no political correctness. At the end, I kept having to grab reporters and remind them that they didn't know what the story was until they got out there and found it."

And when they found it, the goal was to bring their powers of observation, analysis, and perspective to the issue and tell a story.

Tell them what you saw, what someone told you, what you smelled, what it felt like, what they were wearing. Was it cold? Did it hurt? What did you hear? I mean, I was real good at that. I would talk about body language. I would go to hostage situations and say, "I think it's going to be OK." The cops had pushed the hats back on their heads, and they were smoking. That to me was always a sign that they had stepped down from DEFCON 2 to DEFCON 4. And people told me those were great images. I'd spent a lot of time with cops, and I saw that when they put their hats back, and they started smoking and clustering and bullshitting, you knew that they weren't scared anymore. So that to me was the easiest part of my job.

---

1 Danny Meenan: For decades a reporter on various New York City newspapers, he spent many years (until his retirement) as a street reporter for WMCA Radio in New York. He died in 1997.

2 Pete Hamill: Noted author and columnist and one-time editor of the *New York Post*.

Very often the best stories seem rather obscure when you start out. I won many awards for doing stories the boss thought no one would be interested in. One example is a story I did on "sick building" syndrome. The term, referring to bad air in buildings making workers sick, was virtually unknown at the time, and yet it affected millions of people every day. We called the series "Take Two Deep Breaths and Call Me in the Morning." We offered pamphlets and other materials to those who were interested. Within a week we had gotten over six thousand requests. Not bad for a story no one cared about.

The same thing happened when I did a series on Lyme disease when little was known about it, or rabies, which had just re-emerged in raccoons in the Northeast. In that series, called "Killer on the Loose," we emphasized that since this outbreak of rabies was new to the area, people were not prepared to deal with it. Their pets weren't vaccinated. Their kids hadn't been warned to stay away from strange animals. A health commissioner from Long Island called me as the series began airing. "Why are you running this?" he snapped. "It's just sensationalism! There hasn't been a case of rabies on Long Island for more than two decades. Why are you trying to frighten people?"

"That's just the point," I explained. "Because it hasn't been around for almost thirty years people don't expect it, and maybe we have to frighten them a little to get their attention. Rabies kills!" I reminded him. He said I was being ridiculous and indulging in trash journalism. He reminded me again that there was no rabies on Long Island.

A month later, raccoons on Long Island began to attack domestic pets. The raccoons themselves were dropping like flies. Long Island lawmakers passed an anti-rabies law. It required people to get their pets vaccinated, and it also advised people to keep an eye out for those potential killers, rabid raccoons. Incidentally, by the time it was all over, almost 80 percent of the raccoons living in the Northeast had died of rabies. So had some pets and at least one child.

THE ACID TEST

Some stories lend themselves naturally to my acid test. That test is comprised of two words: "Who cares?"

News directors are often moved to ask, "Is it relatable?" In other words, will anyone relate it to themselves and their own circumstances? I have found over the years that people may listen to the news because they think they should, but what they really want to hear is, "Why should I care? How does this affect *me*?" In the end, it seems, the entire world focuses on self and family. But the important point here is that no matter what the story, you can make it relate to your audience. All it takes is a little thought.

In the early 1990s, I was doing a commentary segment called "The Athens Angle" on CBS Television a couple of times a week. At the time, there were serious and tragic goings-on in the world that seemed to hold little interest for the average person and hence garnered relatively little news time, particularly on local TV newscasts. I was determined to find a way to make a bleak news story a relatable one. It went like this:

Bosnia, 2/10/94

A wise old man of television news once gave me some advice. "If you are going to do commentaries," he said, "don't do them about foreign issues. Nobody understands them or cares about them." In the past few months, I don't know how many times I've heard editors in newsrooms look at a Bosnia story and say, "Bosnia? Nobody cares about that! Let's lead with Joey Buttafuco or Tonya Harding"—or whatever that day's "hot" story happened to be.

Trouble with Bosnia is, it's hard to keep track of who the bad guys are, and there are no clear-cut solutions. Americans can't shout things like, "Go get 'em!" Go get whom? Well, we point out, it appears that at this time the Serbs are the bad guys, the Croats are not so bad, and the Muslims are caught in the crossfire in Sarajevo. I know this hasn't helped pique your interest, so let's relate it to you.

Suppose every time you went outside, you didn't know if you'd ever come back home or if there would be a home for you to come back *to*. Maybe you'd lose one of your kids while he was out foraging for some scraps to eat. You've probably already burned all your furniture for heat. Some of you haven't left your apartments for months—not gone outside at all for fear of dying. And maybe, as one ten-year-old did in Sarajevo, *your* ten-year-old will tell you, "Mom, I hope I get hit by a bomb. I don't want to live this way." It happened!—and all of this because you happen to be of a different ethnic background from the guys who live in the hills above you, who have decided to wipe you and your kind out. And in Europe, some newspaper editor is looking at the newswires and saying, "U.S.A.? That's boring! Got anything new on the Princess?"

I'm Art Athens with the Athens Angle.

THE BLANK PAGE

It's actually easy to cover a specific story that has been assigned to you. It's far more difficult to be told by an editor, "Go find a good story and have it in by five o'clock." Assigned stories mean you don't need any ideas. Being left on your own means you begin each day with a blank page. That was worrisome even to the master of storytelling, Charles Kuralt.

Nobody ever gave us an assignment in all those years. I really developed, as an article of faith, that we would find something. I was worried about it at first, but though we always had an idea we were headed toward on the road, we kind of hoped we wouldn't get there—that we would stumble upon something more interesting along the way. And we frequently did that.

For example, one time we were in Ohio, rural Ohio, driving along, and we saw a big sign stretched between two oak trees in the yard of a farmhouse that said, "Welcome Home, Roger," and we passed by it. I looked at Izzy, he was driving the bus that day, and he looked at me. Without a word, we stopped and turned around to go back to see who Roger might be . . . because we had learned that it's easy to drive right past stories if you don't stop and talk to people. Go to the trouble—it will only take a few minutes and it might turn out to be something. Well, Roger turned out to be a GI who was coming home from Vietnam. They didn't know exactly what day he was going to get there, but he was on leave and he was coming home and his mother was actually in the kitchen, baking a cake. It was Roger's favorite kind of cake, and his wife was there with a baby he hadn't seen yet. It was just almost too good to be true.

So I said, "Do you mind if we come in with cameras and talk to you all for a minute?" And his mother said, "Well, let me fix my hair . . ." I bet we weren't there forty-five minutes, and we never did see Roger.

It was just a story about waiting for Roger, and the excitement of anticipating his coming home. And I wrote it that afternoon as we drove on up the road, and we recorded it that night: "Waiting for Roger." Somehow or other, that story touched a chord in America. When it went on the air that night, Cronkite introduced it. It didn't amount to much, but the switchboard lit up, I'm told, and I know that hundreds and hundreds of letters came in asking for it to be repeated and all that. It just was a situation that was similar to that in thousands and thousands of other homes. And Cronkite had to go on the air a few days later and say, "Oh, by the way, Roger got home OK," because there was so much interest in it. It's that kind of thing: Just . . . don't pass things by. They may turn out to be something.

Kuralt told me he knew in his gut when he sent it in that it was a good story.

I felt this was another example of our making something out of nothing, in a way. For example, there was no reaction from Roger. We didn't even see Roger. We left two or three days before he got there. But yeah, when we sent it in, I knew that this was an above-average story.

I had to ask Kuralt what one of his favorite stories was, and did the way it turned out surprise him?

We did a story . . . I thought of this when you said, "surprised you, came out better than you thought it would." We went down one Thanksgiving Day . . . and that's another bit of advice to young people: Forget about all those family holidays, pal. You're going to be somewhere else!

Anyway, one Thanksgiving we went down to a house, a black family's house in Mississippi. One of the daughters of the family had written a letter to tell me about this. It was their parents' fiftieth anniversary, and they had eight children and they were all coming home with *their* children to visit their folks on Thanksgiving to celebrate the anniversary. And I thought, well, it's a family reunion, that's all. We'll go and do a family reunion. Well, it turned out to be some family. I mean, these people were so poor, when the oldest boy decided he wanted to go to college, all his folks could do for him was hitch the mule to the wagon and go to town and borrow two dollars for bus fare from one of her relatives. And that's all they could give him, the bus fare to get there. Well, from that beginning he became Dr. Cleveland Chandler, who was chairman of the Economics Department at Howard University. Each of his younger brothers and sisters, helping each other, had similar successes. I mean, they all went on to earn college degrees and advanced degrees, and one is a minister in Denver, one was a Veteran's Administration dietician in Kansas City, and they were all successes in American life. I mean, *resounding* successes—and here they had all come back to the new house they had built for their parents with their success. And they hadn't been together, all of them, since they were little kids. And Mr. Chandler couldn't get through the blessing at the . . . you know, he started weeping. And *I* was weeping.

I looked over and everybody in the room . . . Izzy couldn't see through the viewfinder. And what were we crying for? We were crying for this, I guess, this cliché, this notion that if you really want to succeed badly enough, this country does give you an opportunity. I mean, they proved it by just starting with nothing and making it themselves, with the encouragement of their folks. It ended with Mr. Chandler playing the old upright piano and everybody singing. Somehow or other, it was a heart-lifting story, and they [CBS] let it run. And I became an honorary Chandler. They send me all the messages about all the things that happen in their families. But I went to hear one of the grandchildren play the violin at Carnegie Hall last year, too. Now the family's extending into new generations, expanding out into America, and all of that beginning with two dollars for bus fare. It still sends chills down my spine to think about the Chandlers.

So an open mind in approaching what was to have been a simple reunion story turned into quite a moving saga.

That's it. You frequently find that the story you went there imagining you were going to cover is a different story entirely—or almost entirely. It often requires a different approach, and what you thought maybe was going to be an amusing story turns out to be a touching one, or vice versa. That is true—and I had to learn that. I had to stop trying to make these stories fit my idea of what they were going to be. I had to just let them happen.

Kuralt observes from experience that a story well told is a story long remembered, no matter how it weighs in on an editor's news scale. To many, there has to be a bomb or a body to make it a "real" news story. "Well," Kuralt says,

> It's also a story when an old woman teaches herself to carve fiddles and does so, to good effect. Good fiddles . . . in the Ozarks. I daresay people will remember that old woman when they've forgotten whatever other important news, so-called, was happening that day. People will see me on the street or in an airport or something and say, "Well, I'll never forget that story about the guy who built a yacht on his farm in Iowa." You know, that was twenty years ago. They couldn't tell you what the big news of that day was, but they remember those human stories.

Some might argue that the stories Kuralt did weren't important stories.

> Well, I would never argue that the stories I did were important. I mean, I suppose you could manufacture such an argument, but I . . . I mean, I recognize that the news is on the air for an important reason: This kind of society needs informed citizens to make decisions, and they can't make decisions unless they know what's going on. So coverage of those stories people should know about or have to know about is important. They don't have to know about a man building a road all by himself up in Minnesota. And it doesn't materially change their lives.

Yes it does, Charles. Yes it does.

5

SO WHAT'S NEWS
~DON'T ASK!~

The crusty old city editor relit his well-chomped cigar and forceful-
ly blew a blue-gray cloud of acrid smoke over his cluttered desk.
He was pissed. He had sent his cub reporter to the stadium to
cover the big game, which should have been over for some time now.
Deadline was approaching, and he hadn't heard a word from the budding
young scribe. The now furious editor had left messages all over town.
Finally the phone rang.

"Where the hell have you been?" steamed the editor. "For chrissake,
we've only got a few minutes to get that story in the paper!"

"Don't worry about it chief," the young journalist reassured his boss.
"There's no story, so there's no problem."

"What the #&*%#@*&!!! do you mean, there's no story?" the editor
sputtered. "It was the championship game! What the hell do you *mean,*
there's no story?"

"It's very simple, chief," the reporter calmly replied. "There was no
game. They cancelled it when the stadium burned down."

So what's news? According to my antique, three-thousand-page
Webster's New International Dictionary (1927), the word "news" has
French origins, coming from the word *nouvelles,* as in novelty.
"Something strange or newly happened; novelties," says Webster, which

continues: "a report of a recent event; information about something before unknown; fresh tidings; recent intelligence." The reference to intelligence certainly comes into question in some stories we've seen or heard lately.

My much newer *Webster's New World Dictionary* (1991) defines "news" as "new information about *anything*" (my emphasis), and it seems that in today's world of news, *anything*, indeed, goes. I write all this here just to make a point. Is *anything* really news? And who decides? It seems we each have our own definition. I always say that to be a news story, it must pass the "Who cares?" test. If nobody cares, it ain't worth tellin'.

Linda Ellerbee has her own theory.

"Who cares?" is a good question to ask, but I think we run a risk today of the news lineup [choice of stories] of the program being controlled by the notion of what the people want. Or what somebody *thinks* the people want, or thinks the people at least won't want to miss. And so the basic core of the arrogance goes like this. Most of the people who work in broadcast news really think they're a lot smarter than most of the people who watch or listen to broadcast news. So instead of giving their very best, they are content to give the viewer or listener what they think he or she would want, or needs, or doesn't want to miss.

I don't think our mission is just the "Who cares." I do believe many studies say that most people don't care much about foreign news. So if it's only "Who cares," we would never be telling about the rest of the world. I think the rest of the world is as important as how to grow your own Christmas tree for next year. And there's nothing wrong with that. You can have Martha Stewart over here, you can have *Foreign Affairs* over there, and broadcast news is somewhere in the middle.

It's not original, and it has probably hung, in one form or another, on the walls of most newsrooms in America. It's called a "Newsworthy Proportionality Chart," and it's a tongue-in-cheek guide to determining the importance of a news story. My CBS News colleague Paul Jeffers drew up this one.

200 thousand Pakistanis dead in a typhoon
equals
4,000 Peruvian peasants killed in a landslide
equals
540 Japanese lost as a ferryboat overturns
equals
102 Yugoslavians trapped in a coal mine explosion
equals
41 Portuguese senior citizens dead in an old-age home blaze
equals
4 California tuna fishermen lost in storm
equals
One three-year-old girl trapped in a well in Teaneck, New Jersey

You get the idea. What's of great interest to one is of little interest to another. The fire in the house down the street from you or the accident on the corner near your house might not ever make the local news, but you and your neighbors may talk about it for days to come. It's all relative.

Professional news people think—or, at least, hope—that they have the ability to determine what is of most importance, or at least of most interest, to their readers, listeners, or viewers. Many use the yardstick: "What stories have the most effect on the most people in our audience?"

By that measure, the almost universal conclusion of news directors is that the *weather* is the most important story they can broadcast. Especially in radio and television news—which, unlike print news, are immediate. Paul Conti, news director at WNYT (NBC) in Albany, explains it this way:

> This may be perverse, but as an industry we may be so bad at identifying what's relevant to people on an average day that the most relevant thing we may be doing is the weather—because it's the thing that has the most impact on people, directly on their lives. The rest of the stuff that we're putting in our newscasts, we're either not doing a very good job of explaining to people why they should care about it or relating it to them, or we're not picking the right stories all the time to

make it more relevant. Whereas, by its very nature, we don't have to do anything to make weather relevant. It's relevant because you have to exist in it. It's the environment in which you live. So that's why it's big. Violent weather can destroy the property you live on, or your relatives', or a friend's. It can make you late for work. It can cancel your wedding. There are just all sorts of things that can relate the weather directly to someone's life without us doing anything. I think that's one of the reasons why weather is such a big issue.

Conti says he has degreed meteorologists at his station, and they're paid nearly as much as the anchors. When storms approach, their all-but-gleeful faces can sometimes be seen on the air almost as much as the anchors'. Weather is often the top story.

Many television stations do not have degreed meteorologists but use what are called "broadcast meteorologists," many of whom come from the Broadcast Meteorology Program of Mississippi State University. Each year the director of that program sends letters out to TV news directors introducing the new graduates. He says in the letter:

> We are the only school in the nation that specializes in producing broadcast meteorologists. Our students complete the meteorological courses necessary for seals of approval from both the American Meteorological Society and the National Weather Association. In addition, they complete courses in television production and other courses in which they perfect their on-air skills as broadcast meteorologists.

A broadcast meteorologist is not an *actual* meteorologist but a kind of hybrid, whose credentials are as important to the news director as his or her ability. You may notice the small "Seal of Approval from the American Meteorological Association" logo that is often displayed on the screen. *That* sets a station apart from its competition.

An article in a recent issue of the *RTNDA Communicator*[1] quotes one Midwest news director as saying he has enrolled two of his longtime

---

1 RTNDA: Radio and Television News Directors Association, one of many national organizations dedicated to the broadcast news industry.

weathercasters in the Mississippi State correspondence course for weathercasters, just so they can flaunt the title "broadcast meteorologist" to their viewers. The news director says he doesn't think it will make them "better weather guys." It will just make them *seem* better.

To use a phrase from a classic *Seinfeld* episode: "Not that there's anything wrong with that"—but isn't it interesting that there is a whole school dedicated to making people look good telling us about the weather on TV? It's especially interesting, since they generally get that information from the National Weather Service, where much lower-paid government employees, who probably wouldn't look so good on television, figure out what the weather is going to be.

In addition to weather, news directors' lists of other relevant stories include health, personal finance, and recreation—hardly what some of us would consider *real* news, like wars, politics, and government. They call the first kind of stories "news you can use." Cute, huh?

And some use the yardstick: "What *should* our audience know about? What do they *need* to know?" Some argue that the public should be given a good dose of what it *needs* rather than what it *wants*. So we have *The NewsHour with Jim Lehrer* on public television, which takes an in-depth look at what it considers to be the important world event of the day. It gives far more time and depth to a single story than any network or local TV newscast ever could. As opposed to the school of giving the public what it *wants*—or, at least, what it is perceived to want. Thus, we have the so-called tabloid news shows and gossip shows, which tease us with headlines like the one that introduces this chapter. Do we really need to know what celebrities were doing when they learned of the death of Princess Di? Of course not. Do we *want* to know the answer to that question? Perhaps some of us do. Is it *news*? Based on Webster's definition, one could say it is. It certainly is a novelty.

TOP OF THE HOUR

"If it bleeds, it leads" is a favorite mantra among TV consultants, who say that crime-and-slime stories always attract viewers. It ruled in Orlando, Florida, for years. When Bill Bauman left his post as news director at a Sacramento television station to come to Orlando, he brought with him a great news legacy.

I was the news director at KCRA in Sacramento, probably either the number one or number two NBC affiliate in the country for twenty years. We had eight hours a day of news that we produced. The consultant would say, "You can't do politics, it's boring." I said, "I'm in the state capital. I'm going to have *two* political reporters." We did a lot of contrarian sort of things there, but it was a well-educated audience. Probably 65 percent of our audience worked for government in one form or another in California, and there was a great tradition. I claim no credit for that; I just inherited a great tradition, and for ten years I kept it up. KCRA was, I think, just journalistically— forget ratings, although the ratings were there too—but journalistically was one of the finest local news operations in America for a long time.

So this job [running WESH in Orlando] became available. It was owned by the Pulitzer Company. [Hearst-Argyle now owns it.] The man who supervised this station for Pulitzer had worked with me in Sacramento, and he called me and said, "Would you consider coming back here as general manager?" I went through all the reasons why I thought it was a bad idea, primarily because I'm a news guy; I'm not a sales guy. And being general manager is a lot different from being a news director. "But," he said, "you know, fundamentally, we believe we cannot improve this station's position in the market unless we improve the news content. The market here is awful when it comes to news." And it's true. My mother lives here. I grew up here. I come down once or twice a year, back from California, to play golf with friends and see my family. And I have friends in the market. And I knew that the news in the market had deteriorated to a real tabloid style of local news, driven by the ABC affiliate WFTV, owned by Cox Communications. And they brought true meaning to the phrase, "If it bleeds, it leads." I mean, all the kids were in handcuffs; there were blue lights everywhere; a lot of crime tape.

Bauman's mission, if he chose to accept it, was to turn the station around, one-tenth of a ratings point at a time, if necessary. They didn't tell him that if he were caught they would deny knowledge of his mission, but that is almost implied when such a gargantuan task is parceled out. Bauman took to the challenge with a vengeance. He knew that the ABC affiliate WFTV and its tabloid news format dominated the ratings. Bauman remembers the first time he visited his Channel 2 control room.

I walked into the control room during the newscast, and all the monitors were in the control room. I said, "OK, that's NBC preview, that's NBC air, that's CNN, that's our live path." You're kind of in your mind checking off the monitors, and there's this great big monitor hanging from the ceiling and there's news on it, but I can't figure out what it is. And then Channel 9's [WFTV's] logo comes up on it, and it's Channel 9's newscast. I looked at the producer, and I said, "You've got Channel 9's newscast on in our control room." She said, "Those are our orders. We always have Channel 9's newscast on." So that gave me some inspiration, and I walked out to begin the staff meeting and I looked at the news director and I said, "You have Channel 9 in our control room, and I'm here to tell you, they do not belong in our control room anymore. There's one of two things, take the monitor out or put it on something else, because Channel 9 is never going to be in our control room again." And people went nuts. And, fundamentally, that was what was wrong with the whole market.

Ah, but did they go nuts cheering or booing?

They went nuts cheering. Because Channel 9, by virtue of their ratings strength, set the agenda for the market, and the other stations, the NBC and CBS stations, would watch Channel 9's news show and then run out and chase what they were doing. And it created an awful editorial process. And more important, they were responding, they were not deciding for themselves what was important.

Bauman brought a new kind of newscast to Channel 2 in Orlando, and after a couple of years the ratings were up, and while crime was still a newsmaker, it no longer had to bleed to lead. Bauman brought enterprise reporting and issue-based news stories to the Orlando market. But one man's issue is another man's boring-turnoff story.

Case in point: Bosnia. Bosnia closed the twentieth century as a major human rights story that many compared to the Holocaust and Hitler's genocide against the Jews of Europe. So, we asked Lynn Sherr, if the

American public shows it's not interested in Bosnia (which it wasn't), then what? Do we not *tell* Bosnia?

No, we should *not* not tell Bosnia, and to some extent we should cram it down their throats. Maybe the problem is you need to find a better way to tell that story, or maybe, just like medicine . . . you just have to have it in there. I mean, what are we talking about? We are a global economy. All this stuff that's going on in Seattle right now [this was 1999],[2] which is fascinating, is people with blinders on. People who will not accept, "Hey folks, the world has changed." A 1960s demonstration ain't going to do it. By all means you should protest what you think is wrong. But let's get real. Things have changed. Let's adapt to the change.

Here we are in network television. We're sort of a dinosaur. Cable television stations, in terms of news, are making what we do obsolete in many ways. People don't wait till 6:30 for the evening news. We have to change. *20/20* doesn't appear at the moment, according to our network, to have the luxury of being a boutique once-a-week program, where we can really delve into great stories. We're now four nights a week; we'll probably go to five at some point. We have to react regularly to breaking news. We have to go out and crash stories on a breaking news story. That didn't used to be the mandate of a program like this. But that's what our bosses now want us to do, because we are second. We're trying to be competitive with all the twenty-four-hour news channels. I don't like it, but I'm not going to throw up my hands and say this is terrible, let's go back to the old days. I think you've got to change. I don't know *how* we change; all I'm saying is that I think you've got to take what the realities are and deal with them. And I'm willing to deal with them. I'm not sure we're dealing with them right yet; I think we're in a transition period.

So we come to another crossroads on the trail of a news story. Is it *hard* news or *soft* news? Chances are it won't matter much, as long as it's *breaking* news.

2 Site of the World Trade Organization (Third) Ministerial Conference, disrupted by violent street demonstrations and finally called off.

USED NEWS

One would think that breaking news is always news, but even that depends on perspective. I was once sent to cover an early-morning story where a group of protesters had spread themselves across the inbound lanes of the New England Thruway, a major artery into New York City. Our traffic helicopter had spotted the demonstration from the air, stopping traffic dead. It was just after six in the morning, and cars had already backed up twenty or thirty miles as hundreds of thousands of commuters began their daily trek south from Connecticut to offices in Manhattan.

As first reporter on the scene, I climbed down the steep embankment to the road. The obvious question was, "Why are you doing this?" Well, it seems the protesters were tenants in nearby public housing, where the rents were about to be raised. Politicians ignored them, so they decided to get some attention this way. They got attention all right! Motorists were fuming. When I went on the air the first time at 6:30, I explained what was causing the backup and why the protesters were protesting. I had to leave unanswered the question, "What would it take to get them to leave?" They were vague about that.

Next, the cops showed up in force and confronted the several dozen men, women, and children (yes, even in baby carriages) strung across the road. Some were sitting, some were standing; some were shouting, some were quiet—but all had determined looks in their eyes, and most were waving signs overhead protesting the rent hike.

The cops didn't want to start dragging people away, so the captain in charge asked the leader of the group the same question I had asked them. The answer this time was not so vague. "We won't leave until the TV cameras get here," the leader replied matter-of-factly.

It was now seven o'clock in the morning, and traffic into the city was reaching crisis proportions. I went on the air again, live from the scene. It was a simple story to tell our listeners, many of whom were sitting still in those miles of traffic, wondering if they would ever get to work or if they should turn around and go home.

The story went on the air something like this:

♦ Who was there? *Protesting tenants objecting to a rent hike.*

+ What effect were they having on traffic, etc.? *Jammed all the way into Connecticut and now affecting alternate routes as well.*

+ Why were they there? (Tape of protest leader.) *They felt it was the only way they could get attention for their plight.*

+ What were the cops doing about it? (Live interview with the captain in charge.) *They were not going to force the people off the road at this time.*

+ How did motorists already stuck there for almost an hour feel about it? (Tape of irate motorist.) *Pissed off!*

+ Finally, the answer to the most important question: When will this nightmare end? The answer was a simple one. I announced to the world: *The police have decided to take no action at this time, because the protesters told them they would leave as soon as the TV crews got here.*

I signed off. My two-way radio crackled. "The boss wants you to leave the story and come right back to the station," said Senior Executive Producer Lou Freizer.

"Are you kidding me?" I sputtered. "This story is just getting going. I can't leave."

"He says he wants you to drop the story. Period."

The tone of Freizer's voice told me it wasn't a joke. Mystified, I climbed back up the embankment to my car. As I headed back, I learned why the boss wanted me off the story. He was exclaiming on the air that our radio station "would not be used by any group to gain publicity for itself." I was torn between crying and laughing. And the ensuing nine o'clock confrontation I had with the boss never resolved the matter. I argued that all media were used all the time by everyone.

Each press release from City Hall, each politician's news conference, every business media event: They were all using us to get publicity for themselves. Perhaps the motives were different in each case, but the goal was always the same. I also argued that we used *them*—for without them, we would have no sources, no news. We might have to actually *work* for a living. Most important, I argued, it was affecting tens of thousands of people. It was *news!* He didn't see it that way. Others were drawn into the argument. It was a stalemate.

Some years later this whole story came up again when I got into a conversation with Mike Wallace about a controversial piece he had just done on Doctor Jack Kevorkian for *60 Minutes*. Known as "Dr. Death," Kevorkian had provided Wallace with videotape of an actual assisted suicide. It included powerful images of the subject assuring Kevorkian that he did indeed want to die, and then very graphic pictures of the actual act—the needle hooked up, the injection being administered, the whole nine yards.

My conversation with Wallace went like this:

ATHENS: Just want to get quickly into the Kevorkian thing, which my wife wouldn't watch.

WALLACE: She wouldn't watch it? Why?

ATHENS: She didn't want to see somebody die.

WALLACE: Did you watch it?

ATHENS: Oh yeah.

WALLACE: Were you offended by it?

ATHENS: No. But she said to me afterwards, "Now, would you have run that tape?" I said, "It's a great fucking story. Without question."

WALLACE: Yeah, of course.

ATHENS: But I've heard a lot of people say that it wasn't really news. I guess that's what I'm driving at.

WALLACE: It wasn't news? Then why is everybody printing it on their front pages across America?

ATHENS: But that's after the fact. *Before* the fact, what made you decide—I realize it's an editorial decision—but what made you say, "Wow, this is a great news story," as opposed to, "That's disgusting, we won't run that."

WALLACE: For the same reason that, when your wife asked you whether you would have run it, you said, "It's a great fucking story." That's exactly the way I felt. It was a great fucking story.

ATHENS: So what makes a news story, as compared with something that Jerry Springer would do, for example?

WALLACE: It is something that makes the reader or the listener or the television watcher . . . makes them . . . it makes the audience's jaw drop.

ATHENS: That's a good news story? Or this particular one? In other words, I got into the discussion with somebody about what is news. The trend today seems to be to survey viewers and ask them what they think news is and then present that to them.

WALLACE: As far as I am concerned, what is news is something that is out of the ordinary. And this certainly applies to the piece that we ran last night. It is something new. The debate is now perhaps more publicly joined than it has been in the past.

ATHENS: OK. One more question. I was called off a story once because people were blocking the Thruway coming down from Connecticut. [I reiterated the story about my boss saying he didn't want to be "used."] Do you feel used?

WALLACE: Used? Of course we were used last night. We're used all the time by people who have a cause, by people who feel, "Dammit, I'm not going to take it anymore." We're used by people who burn the American flag, or who hang Uncle Sam in effigy, or during Vietnam there were so many demonstrations. During the Civil Rights revolution, so many demonstrations. We're being used by people to say, "Look, we have something on our mind. We want to bring it forcibly to the attention of the American people." What better way than to get *60 Minutes* interested? Not necessarily on our side, but simply to reflect that there is a body of thought out there that believes that this particular thing deserves attention. There's no doubt about the fact that Jack Kevorkian used us. I said as much in the piece with him when I said, "What you're embarked on here is a macabre kind of publicity-seeking undertaking to expound on your feelings about euthanasia." He acknowledged it. Nothing wrong with that.

ATHENS: And nothing wrong with the news media playing along, so to speak?

WALLACE: It's not a question of playing along. If the cause is worth it. If it is a serious cause. If it is something that we believe the public should learn more about, by all means.

And it was this belief in the public's need to learn more that shaped Wallace's now-famous interview with Iran's Ayatollah Khomeini.

Here are the hostages; they have just been taken. We have been told that we will have twenty minutes with the Ayatollah. And the first question, by the time it was translated and the answer came from the Ayatollah, which was about ten minutes long—I suddenly realized this may be a one-question interview. Well, fortunately, he sat there and it went on for an hour and fifteen minutes. We had been instructed that we had to submit all the questions in advance or else there would be no interview, and all the questions had, in fact, been submitted in advance. Unless we had done so, we wouldn't have gotten the interview. So finally, toward the end . . . I had this in my notes and I thought, "What are they going to do? Throw me in jail? Execute me on the spot, if I were to ask the unexpected, the unauthorized question? So I said, "Forgive me, Imam." He hadn't looked at me for an hour or so . . . he never made eye contact. "Forgive me, Imam, but Anwar Sadat says you are a lunatic." And the translator looked at me as though I were a lunatic if I thought he was going to translate that to the Ayatollah. I said, "I'm telling you, I saw this on television." So he translates. I had not planned it. I really had not planned it. And all of a sudden, the Ayatollah, for the first time, looked me in the eyes, smiled, and proceeded to eviscerate Sadat orally, suggesting that he was . . . hardly a good Muslim for having said it. And that, perhaps— I forget the exact words—but that perhaps that was a situation that would right itself. And, of course, it wasn't a long time later that Sadat was assassinated.

I asked Wallace, "Do you think maybe indirectly it led to that? I don't mean your interview, but his remarks?" Wallace answered, "I think that, in effect, he took on Anwar Sadat and he took him on in a climate . . . in a fundamentalist climate that was building in that part of the world at that time."

NIELSEN RATINGS HORROR: THEY KNOW WHERE YOU LIVE!

Television stations pay money to the A. C. Nielsen Company in exchange for ratings information. For a fee, they find out how many people are watching their programs. With a little extra effort and money, they can also find out where the people who are being measured live. They can get a listing of where the Nielsen meters are in their viewing area, by zip code.

Now, what would you say if I told you that the news stories your local TV station covers depend in some measure on where the Nielsen ratings meters are placed in your TV stations' coverage area. Not on the merits of the story. Not on some educated judgment by a journalist. There are many markets where whether to send a crew to a story is determined by looking at a map or a list of zip codes. The zip code lists tell the news management people where Nielsen is checking home TV viewing habits with meters attached to TV sets. They're not supposed to have that information, but they manage to get it by hiring the right consultants, who then manage to get it in some fashion from Nielsen and pass it on to station management. The consultants get it under the guise of checking where Nielsen is metering so they can make sure their client station is getting a fair shake. Obviously, what the station really is getting by spending enough on the right consultant is an unfair advantage. What's more, the news audience watching that station is not always getting the news it *should* be getting.

Former CBS news executive Dean Daniels puts it this way: "The bottom line is you have to define what our business is—and, from a corporate standpoint, in television our business is not entertainment or news or public affairs or any of those things. Our business is aggregating eyeballs for advertisers. That's all our business is."

Eyeballs are not counted literally but electronically, with meters that are scientifically placed throughout the marketplace to reflect how many people are watching your particular station at any given time. In smaller markets, select viewers are asked to fill out daily viewing diaries with the same goal in mind. It's called ratings. We all know about them, and newspapers follow them hungrily like ball scores and stock prices.

And again, in order to boost ratings, some news management people feel you have to go where the eyeballs are being counted, and not "waste" resources in areas where there are no meters. Case in point: A major TV newsroom in Philadelphia decided not to send a crew on a seventy-minute trip to cover what turns out to be a story of national interest: A ten-year-old boy stabbed his father to death.

When the assignment editor came into the newsroom and asked why a crew hadn't been dispatched, he said the news director told him matter-of-factly, "There are no [Nielsen rating] boxes out there. It isn't worth covering." An uproar in the newsroom caused the station to at least get some tape from another station and run the story. But the rationale for not covering it was, "We want to do stories where people have boxes, so we can increase our ratings." It's that simple. Conversely, they were reluctant to "waste resources" doing stories where there weren't any boxes.

At this particular station, says my source, a bureau was set up in an affluent area where they knew Nielsen placed a lot of meters. But an equal distance away on the other side of Philadelphia, he says, "where there were very few boxes, we would decide not to go, because there were no boxes." It wasn't even a discreet secret, says the source. The news director would yell across the room, "Why should we go? There are no boxes there."

Areas with no Nielsen boxes are often all but ignored, says one assignment editor. Zip codes are required to be placed on assignment sheets next to proposed story coverage for the day, and those assignments are reviewed by the news director to see if the stories will "rate" well—in other words, will they attract viewers who are being counted by the ratings meters. In at least one Los Angeles TV newsroom, a map hangs in the conference room where the morning assignment meeting is held each day. Color-coded pins on the map show which areas in the coverage area have the most meters. You can guess where the most coverage goes. Nielsen would probably prefer no one did this, or at least that no one knew about it. Shhhhh. It's not news; it's a well-guarded secret.

STORY LINES AND BATTLE LINES

Whether it's "hard" news or "soft" news or breaking news, and no matter what the zip code, good reporters often find that they have to fight for their stories. Fight to get permission to even look into an idea. Fight to get the time to research the story. Fight to get the crew to shoot the story. Fight to get enough airtime to *tell* the story. It doesn't matter who the reporter is, how famous or how competent. It's almost a tradition. Good reporters have to fight for every inch of precious ground they need to tell a story they think needs telling. I fought with my bosses. Mike Wallace says he gets into some humdingers with *his* boss.

Lynn Sherr (from ABC's *20/20*) says sometimes you have to fight *not* to do stories.

I think the pressures on us are such that sometimes there's that hole to fill. There's a lot of airtime. I don't do those stories. I don't want to do the coping stories. I don't want to do how-your-two-year-old-behaves stories. Some people seem to like them. Well, that's fine if they like them. We're also sort of redefining news. But, yeah, I still think we should be there doing the Bosnias. And by the way, we were in Kosovo. *20/20* was in Kosovo when that was all happening. I think we should do more. I lament the fact that we're not doing more international news. I think it is terribly insular of us to be only looking inside at this point, which is what we're doing more and more.

It's very hard for me to do an international story unless I find a U.S. connection.

And I think that's wrong. I think we should be doing things all over the world. What is happening to viewers who turn on the TV and learn something? Not because they've been polled or focus-grouped to death, but because, "Hey, I didn't know about that—that's really interesting." We don't do enough of that.

I asked Sherr about fighting the good fight. "On a scale of one to ten, how hard is it to sell a story you think should be told, that they say nobody cares about?"

LYNN: Ten.

ATHENS: Ten?

LYNN: That's a ten.

ATHENS: How hard do you fight for it?

LYNN: It depends on the story. Sometimes extremely hard, if I really care. Sometimes I'll give in, if I haven't got the energy that day or that week or that minute.

ATHENS: How often do you win those bouts?

LYNN: Not often enough . . . not often enough. A couple of years ago, I don't know if you remember, there was a fire in a toy factory in Thailand, and a number of workers, almost all female, were killed. I read the story and I thought Triangle Shirtwaist fire[3]—the doors were locked.

3 Triangle Shirtwaist Company fire: Worst factory fire in the history of New York City, on March 25, 1911. One hundred and forty-six women were killed, mostly workers trapped in the blaze because of blocked fire exits.

It was the Triangle Shirtwaist fire all over again, and I discovered that, thank goodness for me and for our viewers, I believe there was a connection to the U.S. They were manufacturing toys for some American companies. It took a while, but I got the story approved. We went over there—it was a terrific piece.

ATHENS: To stretch your memory a little bit: What was the argument against that story? That's a fabulous story.

LYNN: It's always the same arguments. Will enough people care? Will we get viewers to watch? Will it engage them? At 20/20 we care about engaging viewers. That's fine—I'm happy to engage. Plus: How expensive is it? Money's an issue. How much does it cost us to go halfway around the world to do one thirteen- to fourteen-minute story? Those are the main arguments. And I came back with an argument that this is—I believe it was around Christmas time—so I got to say this is about your kids' Christmas toys. So we won that one. But I lose a lot as well.

ATHENS: Then again, you have to know which fights to fight.

LYNN: Absolutely true. Yeah, I'm a grown-up. Twenty years ago I probably would have gone crashing through the window on every story, or every time I got turned down. But I'm a big girl now. I can say, "OK, I lost that one, but I'll try again on this other one."

Big *boys* don't cry either when it comes to fighting over stories—either *for* them or, as is sometimes the case, *against* them. Take *60 Minutes*'s Ed Bradley:

> You know, I went all the way to Burma on a story. And while I was there I had serious misgivings about what we were doing. But you keep struggling, swimming against the tide. I mean, it was clear to me that, "Wow, we got a problem here. I'm not sure: What is this story?" The producer said to me one day, I think the third day into the story, "OK, today we'll shoot the conclusion stand-upper," and I said, "What's the conclusion? I haven't come to any conclusion. I mean, we've been in Rangoon for three days. We haven't seen anything outside the capital city. So how am I going to draw any conclusions about this story?" I knew we were in deep trouble. But, you know, we kept pushing against it and swimming against the tide, and we came back and did our best to put a piece together. We showed it to Don

[Hewitt] and Don looked at it, and after a long silence he said, "You know, I've never seen a piece I didn't think I could make better— until I saw this one. All you've got here is, "Hey, here come the monks . . . Oh, hey, there *go* the monks. Hold on, here come some more monks." The story never made air, because there was no story.

I can remember many times, going out to a story scene and finding there was no one there, no story. The producer would literally say, "Well, do a story anyway, you're on in five minutes." A classic tale of that comes from Dean Daniels, about a storm when he was producing the eleven o'clock news on WCBS-TV in New York.

> I think it was a December or January day. We were under strict orders—because people like weather, that's why they watch television news—that at the first hint of snow, which was obviously gonna paralyze the Northeast because we're not used to snow up here in the Northeast, that we were gonna do round-robin whiparounds. That's where you have reporters in live trucks throughout our viewing area. It would work something like this: One reporter standing on the overpass showing the paralyzed traffic behind him, and you go to another reporter in New Jersey and that person's saying, "Same thing here." You know, "The carnage has begun. People are lying dead in the streets." [Dean's being facetious, of course.] And you just whip around the tri-state area just showing everybody how bad it is. I guess there's some feeling of community built out of that. We all know that everybody else is in the same deep, dark hole that we're in.
>
> The problem is that it didn't snow. But that didn't stop us from doing snow coverage, because we had already built all these graphics and animations, and there was Snow Watch 1980 or whatever, and we were gonna do it. And it didn't matter if it didn't happen, we were gonna do it. We had promoted it, it was gonna happen. We argued and argued going into the eleven o'clock news that this is stupid: We got five people standing out there and there's nothing happening. Because apparently, as nature does sometimes, the storm got pushed to our south, and it was snowing on the fish in the Atlantic but it wasn't hitting people. "No! We're gonna do it anyway, cause that's what we're supposed to do. People care about the weather." But even all the

arguments about, "Don't you think this is sort of a 'Boy crying wolf' deal here, where we say it's going to do something and it doesn't? Don't we look silly, and after a while don't people not listen to us when we make the same claim again?" "No! We're doing it, we're doing it." So we basically tell the reporters, "Look, keep this as short as possible. As painful as this is, and as stupid as it is, just keep it short." So it was like, we went thirty-five seconds, boom, boom, boom, all five of them standing on these rain-soaked roadways talking about how lucky we are that the snow passed us by!"

That's thirty-five seconds times five people. That's a lot of time.

That's a lot of time. Well, you gotta justify why you're there. "I'm here," boom, boom. By the time you get there, it's like, "They were ready, they had the salt, but they'll use it for their mashed potatoes," I don't know. So we go through this whole process, come off the show, we're done with the broadcast, we get a message. The boss has called. He wants us to do a cut-in at 11:45 for anybody who may have tuned in late or missed our coverage at the top of the news and let them know that, I guess, if the snow should turn around the next morning and hit us while we're sleeping—do a sneak attack on us—that we'll be there with coverage in the morning. I'm thinking, "You're kidding me." So we grab an anchor and say you gotta stay, we gotta do a cut-in.

So we do our cut-in and we're starting to walk out, just completely demoralized, three guys who have basically spent ten years building a career out of what they thought was something to be respected, and here we were doing . . . just garbage. I'll never forget Randy [Joyce, news producer]. We walk out, and across the street they have that electronic time-and-temperature gauge, and nobody's saying a word. We walk down from the second floor; nobody's said a word. We're gonna go out and get a beer. We look up; the time thing says 11:57. I'll never forget it. It flashes from that to the temperature—48°—and we're looking around and the ground is wet and Randy, you know, very dryly, says, "We gotta go back in." I say, "Why?" He says, "We gotta get on the air." I say, "What are you talking about?" He says, "Suede shoe alert!"

THE GENTLE GIANT

Who can imagine a pussycat like Charles Kuralt fighting about a story? But he did. In his own quiet way, Kuralt went into battle with the best of weapons. Quality. Great writing. Irresistible story lines. And a gentle battle cry. His strategy to fight for a story?

> Well, I just did them and sent them in and let them [management] decide whether or not they were a success. That's an advantage that I had over many. Nearly every young reporter has to go out and do what the boss tells him to do and doesn't have a chance to prove that his idea is a good one necessarily. I do remember one fight right at the beginning of the "On the Road" series. The stories were not to be just on the evening news, but were to come in and be used for what they called "net first." Which meant that the first person who wanted to use a story from us and had a show coming up could put it on. It could be on the morning news, or the evening news, or the weekend, or whatever. We hadn't quite figured out what "On the Road" was yet.
>
> I can't remember his name, but there was a young pitcher who the year before had been pitching for a high school, and that day he was starting in a World Series. So I thought, "That really is something." We were near Berlin, Connecticut, that morning and I'd read about this in the paper. So we drove over there quickly; we found his high school coach, and the ratty old diamond where he had played. I stood out on the mound there. (Izzy found a high shot to use, so that we could then dissolve to whatever big-league ballpark it was and watch him walk out to a well-manicured mound a year later.) And, gee, it was terrific. We ran all over town, talking to his folks and his coach as the game progressed, and all over town you could hear the game coming from the radio. The television sets were on, too. It was terrific. It really was a good story, and here's this kid, triumphant in a big-league World Series game. So we quickly wrote it and shipped it. I called the morning news, told them it was coming, and I'm very excited about it. And we all got up early, watched the next morning, and they didn't use it. It just never came up. And I really was upset. I called the producer of the morning news, and he said, "Charlie, I never even looked at the damn thing. We got busy and I'm sorry." But, you see, now it was too late, you couldn't use it that night, because another game had been

played. So I was . . . that's one of the few times I ever got mad in my career, because I knew that that was a marvelous, affecting story. So I called the boss and I told him the story and I said, "They didn't even look at it." And he said, "OK, we'll just send them all to the evening news from now on," because he was sympathetic. He saw that I was right.

So that's how they ended up on the evening news. [Walter] Cronkite wasn't too enthusiastic about it because he, as you know, didn't really love soft feature stories. He thought this was valuable time, and we ought to use it to do something very serious. But he did-n't understand that I wasn't going to do "silly" stories. I was going to try to give us a little slice of American life. And after a while he became a supporter of the stories.

Kuralt felt that not doing "silly" stories was the key to the acceptance and success of his "On the Road" series.

Well, it certainly helped. I mean, I never made fun of anybody; I just couldn't. It always had to be someone I liked or admired . . . We did a couple of amusing stories. There was a family in Idaho with nine children, all of whose names rhymed. I had to just say their names. It was a little, forty-five-second piece. We did some light ones like that, but we never did one that made anyone look foolish or silly. And I see stories like that on the local news every now and then, and it's the reporter being superior, which is just awful, I think.

Kuralt's self-imposed rules of the road paid off in a big way and made him proud.

He found that when you spent your time looking at the human side of things, you had to treat people in a humane way. He had the time, so he took the time.

For one thing, there was no competition at the time I was doing "On the Road." NBC and ABC didn't waste their time with those lit-tle rural stories. The pieces did take a little work, but if I needed a cou-ple of days or longer to finish one I had the time, because there was nobody else who was going to get on the air with it first. And I liked the business of getting to know people a little bit, making friends. You know, most reporters can't go back to wherever they covered a story, because they've had to ask so many embarrassing questions, stick their noses in where they're not wanted. But we, on the contrary, made friends everywhere we went, and we did, I don't know, hundreds and hundreds of stories, so that meant we were never more than a few miles from somebody we had done a story about. We could go back and have a visit, and we frequently did.

Not many reporters can say that, but it's something to shoot for. There's an apocryphal tale about someone who was the target of a Mike Wallace interview for a *60 Minutes* exposé. This guy was behind some sort of scam, and, armed with plenty of solid research, Wallace clearly had the goods on him. When the interview was over, so the tale goes, the interview subject, who had just been verbally and factually torn asunder, stood up, extended his hand to his inquisitor, and said, "Thanks Mike. When will this be on?" Did it really happen that way? It makes a great story, doesn't it? And, as Ed Bradley notes, a great story is in the eye of the beholder.

You know, we don't have a list of things you have to hit here, or measures or standards that have to be met, that you can look and say: Well, this story does this; this story does that. I think it comes down to institutional taste and institutional memory. I think you have a sense of who you are and where you've been, and you recognize a good story. It's like [Supreme Court] Justice [Potter] Stewart when it came to defining pornography; he said, "I know it when I see it." And it's the same thing about a good story. I'm not quite sure how to define it, but I know when I see it."

« How John DeLorean gets off—at eleven »
NEWS TEASE WHEN THE AUTO MAGNATE WAS ACQUITTED ON DRUG CHARGES

6

COOCHY-COOCHY-COO
~MILKING THE BABY~

'**W**hen news breaks out, we break in." I always used to chuckle when I heard that station break news promo on a local TV station. I'd get a picture in my mind of news escaping from some place or other, and of reporters trying to jimmy a door open to get to it. I heard Dan Rather say it recently about the Republican convention, as if there would actually *be* some news breaking out at that highly orchestrated event. In fact, there hasn't been any actual *news* breaking out of a political convention for decades. But I digress.

There seems to be a trend in news today to emphasize the sheer excitement of the medium. Stations are always giving us *live* reports (instead of dead ones?). Interviews are called *exclusive,* if for no other reason than that no other reporters bothered to show up. There seems to be a belief out there that news can be sold to the consumer as important, whether or not it is, just by giving it a special cachet—which is defined in my dictionary as (among other things) "a little wafer enclosing a bad-tasting medicine."

That wafer often comes in the form of a tease—that is, a promotional announcement that entices you to think that you are going to miss something important if you don't stay tuned. I *hate* teases. So does Andy Rooney.

Well, you have to have headlines on stories to attract viewers' attention, and that is the big argument downstairs at CBS News right this minute. You can bet it's the big argument at the newspaper. How big should the headline be? How titillating should the headline be? Should it be factual or should it be just tease? A tease to get people to read the story. In the *Times*, it's factual. In the *Daily News*, it's a tease. Television news, network news, is still at war with itself over how much should be tease and how much should be fact—and unfortunately, in the last ten years, they have gone too heavily toward the tease.

I am put off in a major way when I am told Tuesday night about the big news story I'm going to get tomorrow, Wednesday. If it's news, goddamnit, give it to me today. I don't want it tomorrow, because it's history then.

History, schmistery. The whole idea of teases is—you guessed it—ratings. Teases come in all shapes and sizes. Some begin days before a story actually airs. This happens especially during ratings "sweeps" periods. They go something like this: "Information that could save your life—a special series all next week on *News at Five*." Now, you may not have even been aware that your life was in danger—or, if so, from what. It doesn't really matter, just so long as you're scared enough to say to yourself, "I'd better watch that." They don't even give a hint about the actual topic, because to do so might eliminate some potential viewers. If they say it's about car safety and you don't drive, you won't care. If it's about medical treatments and you're not sick, you won't care. But if it's about saving your life and you don't want to die, you'll care. Get the idea?

WORLD'S MOST NOTORIOUS TEASE DEBUNKED—FILM AT ELEVEN

One of the most notorious teases is still talked about industry-wide, years after it happened. It occurred in the 1970s, in the very early days of so-called "happy talk" news, a creation of ABC-owned local TV stations and the brainchild of news executive Al Primo. So the story goes, a homeless man fell asleep on the railroad tracks, and a train struck him and killed him. In the process, the man's penis was severed. KGO sent a film crew. (This was before videotape, and the reason for the cliché *"film at* eleven.") The film, a close-up of the penis lying by the track, ran in a tease that went something like, "A sick joke, or a tragedy—film at eleven." Thereafter, it is said, KGO came to stand for "Killers, Guts, and Orgasms." A truly great legend, told to me originally by broadcast consultant Don Fitzpatrick.

That story has made the rounds of every newsroom in the country. It has been talked about at news conventions, at broadcaster luncheons, or wherever two or more newspeople gathered. My friends have all told me, "Oh yes—I remember that happening." Only no one seemed quite sure what exactly was said, or how it came about. So we dug up the anchorman who was there at KGO at the time, who said it. His name is Frederic Van Amberg, and here's what he told me.

Van Amberg says it happened at the height of a series of murders in the Bay Area that included the finding of some dismembered bodies and body parts in the Oakland area.

> That night, one of our contacts at the Oakland PD called and said, "We may have another victim." Our assignment editor took the call and asked, "What's it about?" and the source said, "We found a male sexual organ alongside the railroad tracks." I was anchoring the eleven o'clock show, and when I came back from dinner we had a big debate about whether or not we should go with it. So we got hold of a professor of psychology at the University of California and asked him, and he said, "It's probably self-mutilation, but we can't be sure because of all these mass murders that have been going on." So we debated and we said, "Well, hey, if it were an elbow, if it were a wrist, if it were a hand or a leg . . ."—and we went through all the body parts and said, "Would we go with the story?" And the answer was, "Yes, we would, because of the circumstances." So I went on, and the tease that we did was, "A male sexual organ has been found along a railroad track in Oakland."

Van Amberg says there was *no* film at eleven because they did not show the penis, though they did have footage of it in a plastic bag being held up for the camera by an Oakland detective.

As it turns out, just as the psychologist had predicted, it *was* a case of self-mutilation. "They found the guy either the next day or the day after because of our story, and basically he was bleeding to death, and they were able to save him."

As a legendary anecdote about teases, the story loses something when the truth is inserted. I'm sorry, but I feel compelled to do in that old chestnut (no pun intended), especially after Van Amberg begged me to set the record straight, as he finds he has to do all the time.

> Fitzpatrick and others have delighted in telling the story of the penis on the railroad tracks. And not long ago I was at an Academy of Television Arts and Sciences luncheon and there was a guy at the table and he said, "I'm from Chicago and I heard about you. You did the penis on the railroad track." And I said, "I did a story about a male sexual organ, but that story you refer to has been told so many times it isn't even close to the original." It has taken on a life of its own. The perception has become the reality.

Van Amberg, noting the language and content on television and radio today, says with a chuckle, "Today, that story wouldn't even raise an eyebrow. Forget Howard Stern; how about the President?" Van Amberg wonders how the Clinton stories would have even gotten on the air in the days of the penis on the railroad tracks. Better make that the male sexual organ, just to be safe.

A lot of teases occur in those teeny-weeny spaces between commercials and programs. Because they are worded so sparsely—they only have a couple of seconds—it often sounds as if great tragedies could be prevented. "A man is shot to death, at eleven." Well, it's only 9:30. Why doesn't someone do something to stop it?

One of my favorites occurred when auto magnate and accused drug dealer John DeLorean was acquitted in his ghoulishly popular drug trial. The tease went like this: "How John DeLorean gets off—at eleven." Mixing sex with drugs—now *there's* a real tease. As we said, it's all designed to get you to tune in, or stay tuned in. Teases annoy a lot of people, but do they work? We asked WESH, Orlando, station manager Bill Bauman about that.

> Teases are a great source of aggravation because, I would submit, 85 to 90 percent of them don't work. They're poorly written—you

know, they're too "inside." Whoever created it had a great idea that didn't translate well, or the video didn't support it, or . . . I just think nine out of ten teases miss. And so they aggravate people. But since we have gone to [Nielsen ratings] meters, and we do measure quarter-hours, I can tell you I have seen some teases work. I mean a good tease will suck an audience in. I'm a great example of an NBC affiliate: I've got one night a week to hit a home run. It's Thursday night, coming out of *ER*.[1] If I don't do a high 20s share I'm going to get killed, because the other nights are a lot more competitive. So all of us at NBC affiliates know you gotta hit the home run on Thursday night.

You know, when *ER* first came out, the popular thing to do was to say, "Well, let's look at the ratings book." All right, 80 percent of ER's audience is women 25 to 54—that's who your advertisers want, anyway. So you get your medical guy and go out and do a story that's going to appeal to women 25 to 54, put it in your second quarter-hour, make sure it doesn't run before 11:20, and promote the hell out of it all night long.

Why hold the story until after 11:20? Because timing is everything when it comes to ratings measurement.

You've got to get five minutes of a quarter-hour to get that quarter-hour. If you watch me till 11:20, I got you till 11:30 in the book. But if you bail out at 11:18, I don't get you for the second quarter-hour. That's why we have all these meter strategies on how to seduce you to stay another three or four minutes. It's ridiculous.

Bauman admits that teasing can be very frustrating for a viewer.

The news broadcast begins with the tease, "A new cure for breast cancer—that story coming up." You wait. You wade through other stuff you're not interested in. Then comes a commercial break and the promise, "A new cure for breast cancer—the story after this." Yeah—*way* after this. It's only 11:07—and, remember, they're determined to

---

1 "*ER*": A smash ratings success for NBC, which enabled the network to dominate Thursday-night viewing habits. It was considered a very strong lead-in to local newscasts.

hold you there until 11:20. They might even tease the story a couple of times more. By the time it airs, you may be torn between actually watching or throwing something at the TV set. But you're *still there!*

You know why we do it? *Because it works.* I mean, the fact that it irritates and aggravates people is secondary.

I recalled how veteran CBS newsman Douglas Edwards always hated teases, or news promos that lacked substance. For example, if you said, "A recall of tainted meat announced today—details at eleven," that was fine. But if you said, "You may have killer food in your refrigerator right now—details at eleven," that's wrong. Bill Bauman, who spent almost his entire career as a news director before becoming a general manager, says Edwards, and others who feel that way, perhaps don't understand. He says he found he had a lot to learn when he crossed the line from being a news guy to doing what many consider to be, traditionally, a sales-oriented job.

You know, Douglas Edwards was in the news business. He was not in the marketing business. I will tell you this, now that I've been sitting on this side [the business/management side] of the fence for two years: There's a ton of things that newspeople don't know about television and about marketing—myself included. These past two years have been an eye-opening experience for me, because your news—if nobody's watching it, it doesn't matter how good the journalism is. You can do the greatest journalism in the world, and if you're not attracting an audience and nobody's watching, who cares? Your advertisers don't care. Your ratings won't go up. Your audience doesn't care. You might as well be Don Quixote as do brilliant journalism that nobody watches. If you're the reporter and you're doing brilliant journalism, and you do a story and nobody watches—nothing happens. That's the worst consequence of journalism, when nothing happens. You've wasted all your time, and effort, and money. And I, as a station manager, I've misdirected my resources. I might as well go out and do "Killers, Guts, and Orgasms"—because I can't do serious journalism if nobody watches. I won't get paid for it. Journalists have got to understand the absolute importance and value of marketing. The journalism doesn't matter, if there's no audience.

I think what someone with my background can bring to the party is that, yes, we've got to get on the marketing road: We've got to tease, we've got to have nice packaging, we have to have nice graphics, we have to spend a few hundred thousand dollars a year to market our station, or more in the bigger markets. But you've gotta have an appreciation for what it is you're selling, and have an identity and know who you are, and that's not easy in this business. People are so ratings-driven, and they're focused so often on those things that drive ratings, instead of on journalism. I believe good journalism will attract an audience.

So while we may sit at home and see the teases and say it's so much nonsense, Bill Bauman is very proud of this fact: Six months after he took over the NBC station in Orlando, a newspaper TV critic wrote, "It seems that over at Channel 2 they are practicing journalism, not nonsense." That quote, says Bauman, is now Channel 2's mantra.

*« You never are there to judge. You
are just there to understand. »*

ADVICE TO JOURNALISTS FROM AUTHOR/JOURNALIST DOMINIQUE LAPIERRE

7

Is That Fair?

~AN OBJECTIVITY TEST~

Journalist and publisher Joseph Pulitzer's credo for journalists was simple: "Comfort the afflicted, and afflict the comfortable." I know some tough old newspaper editors who use that quote often, and they mean it.

Obviously, doing either of those two things would require a reporter to have a point of view, and to express it. But the public in general, over the years, has come to expect that reporters should have *no* point of view—that they should be intellectual, social, and political eunuchs. Of course that very concept is flawed, for if it were implemented we would wind up with a bunch of uninformed Stepford wives (or husbands) who would be incapable of evaluating fact, bringing perspective, or explaining events—as a reporter should.

No, what the public really wants is *objectivity*, the ability to put aside individual opinions and evaluate situations without coloring that evaluation with personal feelings. It is what we expect judges and juries to do. Do they always succeed? No. Do they try? We hope so. So reporters, too, must strive for objectivity.

According to *Webster's New World Dictionary*, objectivity is the state of being "without bias or prejudice . . . detached . . . being, or regarded as being, independent of the mind." According to former CBS news manager Dean Daniels, however, objectivity is not achievable—not so much because *reporters* can't be objective, but because people in general have trouble with it.

When I ran news operations, I demanded that people stop the facade of objectivity. I think objectivity is an impossible goal. Everybody is *not* objective. We all come up with our own individual prejudices and belief sets that are ingrained in us, based on where we lived, who brought us up, what we've seen, how we've been affected. All that makes it impossible for us to be objective. If you see somebody on the street who's dressed in rags, you're not objective: You judge him. If you grew up in a liberal, union, blue-collar town, you have a perspective on somebody who's a Republican that you wouldn't have if you had been brought up in Darien, Connecticut, with a different background. And that's not to say that it's wrong; it's just that I think that in order to be fair, you have to recognize it. Objectivity presumes that you can drop yourself into the middle of a situation and deliver a story to an audience that will receive both sides of what you have to say, *equally*. There's this side of the argument, there's that side of the argument.

"The problem is," he continues, "the story may leave the typewriter that way, but by the time it hits the variety of people who will receive it differently, based on the fact that *they're* not objective, the story has lost some meaning, because it isn't necessarily fair to *them*."

So a fair and objective story may be deemed anything but by its viewers, because they bring their own prejudices with them as they watch it. People on *both* sides of an issue may deem it unfair and biased. Daniels recalls his days as a cub reporter.

I went down to cover a hospital strike and put the thing on the six o'clock news that night, and I'm sitting there and I'm getting calls. The administrator of the hospital is furious at me; the people on the picket line are furious at me. I'm sitting there and I'm green, very green, and I'm thinking, "Oh man, I just pissed everybody in the world off. I'm done. I'm cooked." And Mark Davis, who was my news director, walked out and he said, "What's the problem?" And I said, "Mark, I'm really sorry. I got everybody pissed at me." He said, "What do you mean?" I said, "The people on the line are pissed at me; the hospital administrator and negotiators are pissed at me. They said I did this, I did that." And he said, "So what you're telling me is, you went down and covered a strike and you got both sides pissed at you?" And I said, "Yeah!" And he said, "Great job!"

Obviously, having everybody "pissed" at you could also indicate you did a lousy job, but the whole idea—the self-test every reporter must take—is, "Was I fair?" More than that is not humanly possible. Are there biased reporters? Of course. Are there reporters with an agenda of their own? Certainly. But that is by design. It doesn't have to and shouldn't be that way.

Advocacy journalism has become almost a trend. You see it especially on the local level. Become part of the story, or at least have a viewpoint. Reporters do it and anchors do it. You hear little editorial words creep into the reports. How *horrible* it is that the mother threw her baby off the roof. A woman's throwing her child off the roof is obviously horrible on its face, but I don't need some anchor or reporter to make that judgment for me. You'll see the anchors shake their heads and say, "Oh, what a shame" or, "Isn't that terrible." I don't need to hear that, and neither do you. We asked CBS's Andy Rooney, whose job it is to give opinions on the air all the time, how reporters and anchors can check their personal judgments at the gate.

It's easy if you're a reporter. I don't think it's that difficult. You know what you're doing, you understand the language, you know what the words mean and what implications each one of them has, and you avoid using the ones that show bias in one direction or another. It's absolutely possible."

Even when an item is *intentionally* biased it can be taken the wrong way, skewed not by the bearer of the item, but by the recipient of it. Case in point: a commentary I did on WCBS-TV in New York. This was *not* intended to be an objective news story; rather, it was my opinion, and clearly identified as such.

It involved the Board of Education's spending half a million bucks to buy a house for a potential schools chancellor it was trying to woo to the job from Miami. He demanded a house as nice as the one he was living in that was provided by the Miami school district he headed. The school board argued that this man, Joseph Fernandez, was by far the most qualified candidate to run the million-plus-pupil district; in order to attract such highly qualified people, they said, New York City had to be competitive with private industry and, therefore, provide a snazzy house in a market where housing was at a premium. Hence my commentary, entitled "A House for Joey."

I appeared on camera in my office—first wearing a sport jacket, which I removed as I spoke, changing instead to a cardigan sweater. It was my attempt at being Mr. Rogers. I delivered my remarks as Mr. Rogers would deliver his to a group of kids. Here is what I said:

Hi, boys and girls. Today is a very special day, because I am going to read you some more from our new storybook. It is not a pretend story; it is a real story. Now some people don't like this story, but we are going to read it anyway.

It's called "A House for Joey." [I held up a book, with an art department–designed title jacket.]

Now you'll remember that the Board of Education wanted Joey Fernandez to come to New York from Florida and be schools chancellor. Joey said he would only do it if the board gave him a lot of money and a great big house to live in—just like he had in Florida. Joey was smart! That's why they wanted him to be schools chancellor.

They looked at a house on Staten Island—but Joey and his wife said it was too far from the office. They looked at dozens of houses in Brooklyn. "Too big," said Joey. "Too small," said Joey's wife.

Then they found one that was just right.

It has five bathrooms and seven bedrooms. It costs a million dollars. Can you say "a million dollars"? I'll bet you can.

Now some people say the Board of Education was dumb to spend all that money on a house.

But, boys and girls, if we want the best chancellor, then we have to pay for him, don't we? If we don't compete with the private sector, we will only be able to attract mediocre people to run things. Can you say "mediocre"? I'll bet there's a good chance you can't. I'll bet there's a good chance you can't spell it, either.

That's why they had to spend a million dollars on a house for Joey. So he can teach you how to spell and read—even words like "excellent" and "good investment," and little words like "last hope."

And all the chancellors from now on will be able to live in that house—we hope happily ever after.

So which side was I on? Whatever conclusion you may come to, I must tell you that I received a flood of mail about that piece, half congratulating me for being in favor of what the Board of Education did, the other half congratulating me for "really giving it to that stupid board."

NBC's Brian Williams says that whether you call it objectivity or just plain fairness, there is never an excuse for not giving both sides of the story.

It should be reflexive. It has to be taught when people are starting out, but it should never be something an editor has to order you to do.

There are few circumstances where you don't have time for a phone call to the other side, but it happens. For example, a late-breaking press conference that has to go right into print or right on the air. In that case, you have to rely on your brains. You have to, for safety's sake, add a paragraph that says, "Despite today's late announcement that the new bridge will be built, environmental groups have long protested its arrival, saying that the spotted sea urchin and its nesting place at the base of the Gitchie-Goomie will be threatened by new construction." The next day, you do a follow-up with the other side.

Andy Rooney agrees that there are times when it may be possible to give only one side of a story.

Yes, but you have to make it clear that you were unable to get the other side. You say, one side failed or refused to return phone calls or something. It's absolutely imperative to present both sides, no matter where you stand on it. Of course it is. And if you don't present both sides, you have to make it clear that you know you have not presented both sides and were not able to, because the information wasn't available to you.

And is it possible to write and present in a way that does not reveal your own personal biases? "I don't try to do that," says Rooney.

But I do think it is possible. I did do that, and I am able to do that. If you are honest and intellectually dedicated to good reporting I think it is absolutely possible, and the best example we ever had in this country was Walter Cronkite. People did not know whether Cronkite was liberal or conservative, Republican or Democrat. He concealed that from people just by being absolutely straight about what he reported. You could not say that about any of the three anchormen today. You know, just from the way they use words. If they call a friend of a president a crony, you know that they are unfriendly to that president, and there are a thousand pejorative little words like that that are used in an editorial sense, particularly by anchormen, that give them away.

The most trusted man in America, Walter Cronkite still views himself as more a newspaperman than anything else. Those were his roots—and he still uses newspapers as an important point of reference. Objectivity and fairness are his stock in trade—paramount, he says, even if you have to swim against the tide. In today's marketplace, with the trend being toward advocacy and self-involvement in stories, what chance is there for a reporter to maintain the highest of standards?

Well, it's obviously a very serious question of the reporter's integrity or the anchorperson's integrity, as opposed to management's concept of what should be done. This is not necessarily a new battle between reporters and management; it has gone on in newspapers for years, probably ever since Peter Zenger[1] declared the right of a free

1 John Peter Zenger: Began publishing an anti-establishment newspaper in 1733. His imprisonment and subsequent acquittal on charges of seditious libel marked a landmark battle for freedom of the press.

press in this country, and maybe since the invention of the printing press, to one degree or another. A reporter can hope or an editor can hope to work his or her way up to newspapers of record like the *New York Times*, the *Washington Post*, or the *Los Angeles Times*. But even there, the reporter has to yield sometimes to editorial opinion or the editor's opinion. The editor's opinion sometimes has to yield to ownership opinion. The better papers, the ones with a better reputation, get those reputations because they have little of that, at least not much of it that is transparent to the public. Broadcasting has disappointed me from my earliest days in radio way back in 1935, 1936, when radio was still a fairly new medium. After all, it had only been on less than fifteen years, and all the news was a fairly new thing.

"Why has it disappointed you?" I asked.

It disappointed me because there is very little editorial supervision in radio. I've found that to be true anywhere I've worked, including CBS. There was more at CBS than one or two local stations I've worked at. But even at CBS, there wasn't the kind of editorial supervision you get on a newspaper—even a small, very localized newspaper. The city editor, the copy editor, the telegraph editor—they had authority and they read every darn word of copy, and they changed it and made sure it was right. They were constantly screaming out through the city room the name of a writer or reporter or getting him on the telephone, and complaining about this line or that line and the correctness of it, and constantly getting the most out of the wordage used. I haven't seen that on radio and television desks anywhere.

Ever?

No. Not really . . . the best we had, we had a couple of good editors on the *CBS Evening News*, John Merriman and Ed Bliss. Eddie Bliss—very, very good. And they were better than anybody else, and that was partly, I think, because the whole atmosphere of the *Evening News*, at least with me as managing editor and with them as the editors, was more that of a newspaper than a broadcast. That was my whole approach to the thing. I've always had much more admiration for print than for broadcast, and I carry that with me. I still do.

Why, you may ask, would you need all those editors watching over things when you have a fleet of competent, professional reporters? Does this mean that reporters can't be trusted?

We wonder if the editors of the *Washington Post* asked that question back in 1981 when their Pulitzer Prize–winning reporter Janet Cooke admitted that she had made up "Jimmy's World," the story that won the Pulitzer. Cooke admitted that there was no "Jimmy" and that she had concocted a composite character of child addicts. Her story was, in fact, *not* fact at all. She'd made the whole thing up.

That incident led to a television program on PBS hosted by Hodding Carter, former press secretary to President Jimmy Carter. To this day, I remember distinctly the remarks Carter made at the end of the broadcast, concerning the Cooke fiasco. Carter opined that this proved that editors weren't doing their job, and that it was time that editors took their reporters to task, scrutinizing their every word and virtually tracing their every step in gathering a story.

My thought when I heard that was along the lines of, "Since when do we transfer the responsibility of a reporter to be truthful and diligent to a desk-bound editor? Should not reporters be held responsible for their own actions?" Carter, it seemed, was blaming editors for the lack of ethics in a reporter. Then why not blame her parents, or perhaps the personnel department for a less than probing job interview? It just didn't sit right with me.

BOND (NOT JAMES)

My father always told me, "Son, as you go though life, remember this: Your word is your bond. It is your reputation. It is the one thing no one can take away from you, unless you let them." I learned that lesson well, and I hope I've successfully passed it on to my own children.

I have found that "bond" challenged frequently in life, often in connection with job-related issues. One incident comes to mind that really challenged me. I had made arrangements with the pickpocket squad of the New York Police Department to travel with a team of undercover cops working the midtown area during the Christmas season. The cops were getting a lot of action. I wanted to show listeners just how vulnerable they could be and just how easily they could be ripped off if they didn't take steps to protect themselves.

The cops were glad to cooperate. The only restriction placed upon me was that if we ran into an incident that they deemed should not be reported—if, for example, it might jeopardize a case or compromise their operation—I would agree not to report it. I agreed. It happens that my reporting of police matters and investigative work over the years had earned me the reputation that I could be trusted. So the deal was made.

It didn't take long on our first day out to find some action. As we walked on Fifth Avenue near Saks, a detective nudged me and said, "Watch that guy." I looked over and saw just an average man walking a few yards in front of us. But when we came to the corner, where pedestrian traffic had come to a halt waiting for the traffic light to change, this average guy reached into the pocketbook of the woman next to him and slipped out her wallet so smoothly she was not even remotely aware of it.

The detective literally leapt into action, grabbing the man by the jacket. He wrenched himself free, knocking the detective to the ground as he fled down Forty-ninth Street. The rest of the team gave pursuit and tackled the guy halfway down the long block. He was winded. They were winded. *I* was winded. I had it all on tape: the detective clueing me in; the man running; the detectives yelling, "Stop, dirtbag," or whatever it was they said; the scuffle; the denials; and the arrest. Dramatic, compelling tape. It would be a great piece. I interviewed the detective. How did he know this ordinary guy was out to rob somebody? "It was the way he looked around," said this central casting–type New York City cop. "While everybody else was looking straight ahead at where they were going, this guy kept looking at ladies' bags. His eyes sifted through the crowd looking for an easy mark. He found one." It turns out that the woman wasn't aware she'd been robbed until much later, when a detective located her and told her. She was lucky, and so was I. I had a great story for my series.

Day two. The cops and I headed out, after they explained to me that Gypsy families seemed to dominate the pickpocket trade in midtown. Gypsies, explained the detectives, worked in teams, usually families—the adults perhaps causing a distraction while the kids took the goods, or vice versa. Team members who actually made the "dip" or snatch would quickly pass the loot to another team member who would be headed in the opposite direction. The item might be passed several times as the team scattered. They were hard to catch.

We trailed one such pickpocket team into Saks Fifth Avenue, where they made the rounds of the ground floor looking for potential victims. They then headed out to Fifth Avenue, and we followed them some more. With our detective team a few yards behind them, the family entered a major midtown cathedral, busy with midday worshippers who were scattered throughout the pews—some sitting, some kneeling—taking a few minutes for a personal visit with God.

The pickpocket team spread out, stepping into various pews up and down the aisle. We stood in the back, observing. Suddenly, one of the "family" reached over the back of a pew and grabbed the bag of a kneeling woman apparently deep in prayer. Feeling safe in such a place, she had just left her bag on the seat next to her, never expecting a need to be on her guard.

The young pickpocket quietly took the bag, got up from her kneeling position, and walked calmly up the aisle. Other members of her family fell in behind her as she passed. When they reached the back of the sanctuary they were greeted by the team of detectives. My tape rolled as they were led outside, protesting strenuously that they had done nothing wrong. But, alas, they were already known to the detectives: They had been arrested before on the same charges. After a squad car and uniformed officers took them in, the detectives and I headed for the station house and the lengthy booking procedures that would follow. It was then, however, that my ethics challenge began.

On the way in, the detective I had buddied up with told me that this sort of thing happened all the time, perhaps hundreds of times a year. Unsuspecting worshipers, letting their guard down in what should be a safe haven, frequently had their purses and shopping bags ripped off. "It's a real problem," he told me.

"What a great story," I said. "When we get this on the air, at least people will be forewarned about the dangers existing even in such a revered place as this cathedral. Who would have thought it?"

"Oh," interrupted the detective, "you can't use that."

At first I thought he was kidding, but it soon became clear he was not.

The police and the church had a kind of agreement to keep all this quiet. Seems the church didn't want to frighten away worshipers, didn't want the church board to decide to close the church to passersby during the week—in other words, didn't want any trouble or bad publicity. The cops were cooperative. I could not use the story, or at least I could not mention *where* the story took place.

"There must be a way around this," I pleaded. "The public really should be warned."

"Maybe you can convince our captain to let you off the hook," offered the detective. I called him. No luck. "Maybe you can convince the church to let you do it," offered the sympathetic captain.

My call to the church got me a simple, not-so-Christian warning. If I identified the church in my story, the church would hold a news conference, deny it, and brand me a liar. Not exactly an endorsement of my plan to warn the public.

So far there wasn't much of a quandary. I had given my word. Those were the conditions of my access to the detective team. I would abide by their restrictions, since, obviously, they weren't going to budge on this one.

My problems really began when my boss asked me how it was going. I told him about the great stuff I had and how frustrated I was because I couldn't name the church in my story.

"You have to name it," he said to me, matter-of-factly.

"I know I should, but I can't. I gave my word."

"I'm ordering you to use the name," he countered. He wasn't kidding. It wasn't a ploy to give me an excuse. I again argued that I could not do so. That's when he threatened to fire me. That's when I told him to go ahead and do it.

I didn't use the name of the church in my story. I did identify it as "a major midtown cathedral." He didn't fire me, but I honestly was prepared to go if I had to. My father's words rang true. My word was my bond. In the end, nothing else mattered.

Fact or Fiction

Sometimes you have to be ready to give it all up, rather than *make* it all up. More than once, after spending days or even weeks investigating a story, I would suddenly come upon a fact that blew the story out of the water or changed it so dramatically that it was no longer worth telling. Had I quit my research a day sooner, I would not have known that fact and could have run a great story. Or I could have just left that fact out, pretended it didn't exist, and pushed ahead. Instead, I would wind up explaining to the boss why I had wasted a lot of time. Good bosses always understood.

All of the big warhorses have similar stories to tell. They have all been to that brink where it was either their integrity or their job on the line. There was the time, for example, when Dan Rather was just a cub reporter at a now defunct wire service.

> They were struggling. They were under tremendous financial pressure. They were trying to stay in business. The people I was working for were good newspeople, and they wanted to do the right thing. But the financial pressures on them were such that not only were they asking—even demanding—mediocrity, but also—and there's no joy in saying this—they wanted corners cut. I'll give you an example. One of their contracts was to go out to what we now call shopping malls. We would go out and talk to people about how they felt about products. This was a news organization that had contracted with a business to do this work. I know that today this would raise ethical questions. But nonetheless, I was working for this wire service, they had struck the contract, I needed the money. They called me and said, "By tomorrow afternoon, we need you to talk to fifty people in various parts of the city about peoples' reaction to this product." I said, "Well, there's a hell of a storm here. Everybody's indoors. I don't even think I can *get* to fifty people in all parts of the city in this weather." They said, "Look, you call me back and have it done." Well, I knew what that message was. It was basically, "Make it up if you have to." Well, it's long ago and far away, it was not a good environment, and I needed the money. I thought long and hard about quitting, and finally, I quit. But I did think an awful long time about it, because while the money was small, given my budget at the time, it was a pretty big decision.

OK, now wait! That's only the tip of the ethical iceberg, Dan Rather quitting a job like that. He could have stopped his story there—not told me any more. It's a good story. But Dan continued,

By the way, don't make that read heroically, because it wasn't. I'm not proud of it. I did it. That is, I made some of it up, phoned it in. Never done that since, but I really felt like hell about it. I did call them back later and said, "You know, I gotta tell you . . ." And they just laughed and said, "Listen, given the circumstances, don't worry about it, kid." But I worried about it a lot.

Now, the reason I tell you that story is that we're talking about ethical behavior, integrity, talking about trying to make it in the business. And particularly when you're starting out, there are a lot of tough calls, and there's no way you're always going to make the right call. And I think that if you make a wrong call, you shouldn't get too discouraged about it. You should learn from it. One of the things I learned out of that experience is that you really need to have clearly in your mind things, ethically, you will do and things you won't do.

It needs to be a short list, 'cause if you make a long list you're going to be in the boss's office every other day. You must have that list clearly in your head, particularly when you begin. These are things that I definitely would do: I will double-source every story; I will take the extra steps to make sure I'm accurate. These are things I won't do: I won't do something that's clearly unethical. You need to have a short list in your head for that. It's a version of what my father always said: "You'd better know where you stand, or you'll fall for anything." And there's a version of that in journalism.

Isn't it interesting how your father's advice almost always seems to steer you right? It's also interesting to note that many of my colleagues have put themselves and their jobs on the line over principle. Not over pay. Not over vacation time or office space, but over principle. Andy Rooney sees it as a rite of passage, because some things are just worth fighting for.

You fight it until the point at which you're going to get fired, and then you decide whether you'd be better off, and everybody else that you're trying to do good for would be better off, if you swallowed this. I think you do have to take some things, and you can let yourself off the hook by considering the possibility that you may be wrong. But I think a person ought to quit every once in a while or get fired. Probably in his life he should be fired a few times or quit. It suggests taking a stand. There are so many places to take a stand. You can't do it every day, but there have to be some times when you take a stand.

One journalist I know who has taken many stands over the years, has quit and been fired and now owns and runs her own very successful production company, is Linda Ellerbee. She spent years in local and network television newsrooms. She has taken her share of hard knocks and learned from them.

I love this story and I tell it because I think it's so important. The key thing for young people to remember—[David] Brinkley had told me this—is, what's the worst they can do? The worst they can do is fire you. They can't put you in a Florida jail. They can't eat you for lunch. The worst they can do is fire you, and there are things worse in our business than being fired. And one of them is to not be able to look at yourself in the mirror on your way to work, because you're going to have to do sleaze journalism.

The term "sleaze journalism" is, of course, subjective. Are shows like *Hard Copy* or *Inside Edition* sleazy? Some news broadcasters consider it "sleazy" when other news broadcasters choose to do commercials. It's a long-running and highly emotional controversy. For most of my career, news broadcasters were forbidden by their stations to voice commercials or to have anything to do with commercial endorsements. It was thought that such activities would compromise the so-called objective appearance of the newscaster. Remember, newspeople are not supposed to have opinions—not even about which soap to use. If it were possible, I suppose, broadcast management would have had logos removed from vehicles used by its newspeople so no one would be able to tell what kind of car they drove.

For some strange reason, *sportscasters* were always allowed to voice commercials and to be spokespeople for products. I guess sportscasting doesn't require any degree of perceived objectivity.

Lest you be confused, on all-news stations like my home station, WCBS in New York, anchorpeople who were on the air for hours at a

time were allowed to read live commercials. The spots were generally pre-
ceded with the disclaimer "The following is a commercial message." This
was done so people would realize they were not hearing an actual news
story. (Don't laugh, some commercials were written deliberately to sound
like news.) These same anchors, who read dozens of commercials on the
air live each day for dozens of different sponsors, *to this day* are not
allowed to record a commercial for money that would be played on another station.

Now there are exceptions to every rule. Since we have already established that broadcasters are in business to make money, it is safe to say
that they never saw an opportunity they didn't like. So when the opportunity came along to let Charles Osgood do commercials for which his
network could charge a premium, the ban was lifted from Charlie's shoulders. It was a great compromise for the network (CBS) and some say a
great sacrifice by Osgood, despite the fact that he gets big bucks for
adding his voice and endorsement—like, "I sleep on a Select Comfort
mattress every night, and I love it" or, "I'm up early every morning on my
Nordic Trak, and it's great."

The whole idea just makes Andy Rooney's skin crawl.

Charles Osgood. I feel so—such mixed feelings about him. I'm just
furious at the network and him for the commercials. I can't stand it.
And it would be hard to say he isn't one of the most talented people
in our business and one of the most charming. But it is absolutely
wrong. He should be fired today.

I was so taken aback by Rooney's strong reaction, I interrupted him to
ask why he found it all so offensive.

Because, if somebody has the job of reporting the facts and he, on
the other hand, accepts money to convince people of something about
which he knows little or which he does not really believe, then his
credibility as a reporter is destroyed.

Using Rooney's logic, that same argument could be applied to taking
speaking fees from corporations that you might eventually have to cover.
Well, what about taking speaking fees?

ROONEY: Listen, everybody has backed off that because of those charges. I don't do any speeches, I speak at colleges now, but I just don't go out to companies anymore. I did.

ATHENS: But now, if you spoke at Monsanto, would that stop you, a year later, from doing a story on Monsanto?

ROONEY: No, but even the appearance of it is wrong, so you can't do it.

ATHENS: Mike Wallace says, "Prove—Show me where any of my judgments have ever been influenced . . ."

ROONEY: No, I think that would be absolutely true of Mike, too. But still, I don't think you can do it.

ATHENS: Just because of the perception?

ROONEY: Yeah, I wouldn't do it. I absolutely wouldn't. I used to do some, and haven't done them in several years. Would not do it.

Osgood himself was somewhat surprised at the tone of Rooney's indignation. His first reaction was to turn the tables on Rooney.

> The fact is that every penny that Andy Rooney has ever made in broadcasting has come from commercials. That's absolutely true, and he knows that it's true. This is commercial broadcasting, and it's hard to overstate the importance of commercials to commercial broadcasting. If he's opposed to commercials or taking commercial money, he ought to go to work for PBS.

Having said that, Osgood pointed out that he was asked by CBS to voice commercials, that he no longer does hard newscasts because of it, and that if he ever were to come into a situation where he had to do some sort of story on a sponsor he had previously endorsed, he would recuse himself from doing so. "What's more," Osgood concludes, "if I endorse a product, I'm actually using it. If I say I drive a particular car, I *drive* it. As for Andy Rooney, it's disingenuous of him to criticize when he has taken so much commercial money all this time."

I personally doubt we have resolved the conflict here, and it will surely continue to simmer as long as money is involved.

Linda Ellerbee counts herself among those journalists who have done commercial endorsements, and yet she agrees to some extent with Rooney.

You know, when I quit the network, and we were starting to get this company [Lucky Duck Productions] going, we were having a hard time persuading anyone that we knew anything about producing. They had no idea that I was a good producer. We had a real tough time, and we had some employees. I did a commercial for Maxwell House coffee to keep the company going. And I did it because my choices were to do a commercial for Maxwell House to keep the company going; to do a sleazebag talk show, which there were a lot of offers for me to do; or to go back on my hands and knees to the network and beg for a job. And I felt the cleanest of the three was the Maxwell House commercial. See, I happen to think that these sleazebags, these sleaze talk shows and the sleaze news shows are frightening because of what they *pretend* to be. With a commercial, there was nobody going to be thinking that this was a newscast. You know, it was what it was. It was me sitting there in a big easy chair next to a five-pound can of coffee.

Always a smart-ass, I remarked that it sure sounded like a newscast to me.

Right. Cause you always deliver the news sitting in the living room, right? In a big easy chair with a five-pound can of coffee. Only the *New York Times* was confused by that, by the way. The *Times* did say that the worst thing was that I tried to make it look like a newscast. [Laughter] But they're weird there, OK?

Yes, it was a big enough deal for that venerable watchdog of society to write a story about it. Did Linda feel it was a big compromise for a journalist to do a commercial?

Yes, I did. I was well aware I'd take a beating on it. I knew what the consequences would be. I made a clean choice, and as it turned out the right one, because within the next six months we got our first documentary and we never looked back, and we helped produce an awful lot of good television since then. But at the time I did that commercial, Sam Donaldson said in a newspaper article, "She'll never work again in the business. No one will ever take her seriously." You know.

And I thought about that the next time I won a DuPont or a Peabody or an Emmy. I would never have done that if I were working as a daily, news-covering journalist. I could never have done it. I did it as an employer. I'm still not proud of it.

While what happened to Linda Ellerbee happened some time ago, the attitudes of many haven't changed over time. After David Brinkley retired from decades as the senior figure of ABC News, he did some so-called "image" commercials for the giant international conglomerate Archer Daniels Midland, better known as "ADM—Supermarket to the World." For that, this man who had given his life to journalism—and is considered among the giants of the industry—was roundly chastised by those who thought such a thing compromised Brinkley's credibility and integrity. The man was *retired*! In his *eighties*! Not doing news anymore. Did it compromise his retirement? I don't get it. Nor the flap over Osgood. Yet, certainly Andy Rooney is not alone in his views, and he certainly is consistent about them. Linda Ellerbee recalls:

Andy Rooney. Andy Rooney went on the air and did an editorial about me when I did the Maxwell House commercial. I was on a book tour just after my first book came out, and I was in Chicago when a young man came up to me and said, "You've been taking a real beating on this Maxwell House thing." And I said, "Yeah." And he said, "I found this, I thought you'd like to see it." And he hauled out an ad from *Life* magazine. That ad is framed on the wall behind you. It was Edward R. Murrow from the set of *See It Now*, doing a coffee commercial. [Points to framed ad] And that's Don Hewitt [Murrow's producer at the time] down in the lower-left-hand corner. And I sent a copy to Andy and said, "I guess you just forgot about this one." So, while I don't think it's a good idea, I wasn't in bad company, was I? I mean, there's the patron saint of broadcast journalism up there.

I wondered out loud what Ed Murrow would have thought of all this today. Linda said simply, "Yeah."

8

WIREITIS (Y-ER-EYE?-TIS)

~AN INFECTIOUS NEWSROOM DISEASE~

Ah, the clangor and clamor of a major metropolitan newsroom. The clattering of the wire service machines. The ratcheting sound of typewriter carriages flying back and forth. The squawking of police radio monitors and two-way radios. And the phones. The constant jangle of the phones. All of it masked by a cloud of smoke so thick you could cut it, and the occasional yell of "Who took my ashtray?" Fingers stained by tobacco and carbon paper. How sweet it was. And my, how it has changed.

Of course, for more than a century, news organizations have depended on news dispatch agencies and, later, telegraph and wire services to bring them the news. Around 1846, a man named Daniel Craig ran a pigeon agency based in Halifax, Nova Scotia. He would have small boats waiting to pick up the London papers from ships making the London to New York run. He'd pick out the best stories, rewrite them cryptically, and dispatch his pigeons, which could fly to New York faster than the ships could get there. Even the *New York Sun* had a flock of news pigeons for a few years.

In fact, around 1850, Paul Julius Reuter organized a carrier pigeon fleet to transmit news dispatches around Europe. In 1851, after the telegraph came along, Reuter founded the news agency Reuters. The telegraph became the news transmitter of choice (you didn't have to feed it), and the clucking of pigeons gave way to the clicking of telegraph keys.

Reuter set the standard for what would become the wire services of today when he sent the following memo:[1]

TO: Agents and Correspondents

FROM: P. J. Reuter

DATE: 1883

RE: Please cover the following:

". . . fires, explosions, floods, inundations, railway accidents, destructive storms, earthquakes, shipwrecks attended with loss of life, accidents to war vessels and to mail steamers, street riots of a grave character, disturbances arising from strikes, duels between and suicides of persons of note, social or political, and murders of a sensational or atrocious character." It is requested that the bare facts be first telegraphed with the utmost promptitude, and as soon as possible afterwards a descriptive account, proportionate to the gravity of the incident. Care should, of course, be taken to follow the matter up."

Throughout time, carriers of news have always raced to be first. It probably dates back to the fastest cave carvers or the fastest minstrels, who would rush from village to village to sing their songs of news. Today it's who has a speed dialer on their cell phone with an integrated Internet connection. Everyone wants to be first.

Sometimes that can be a deadly trap. Witness the cub reporting of the not-yet-CBS News correspondent Charles Kuralt, who remembered this old chestnut emblazoned on rulers used to cut wire copy from the International News Service. It was there to see every time you went to the clacketty wire machine to retrieve some new copy, and it said, "Get it first, but first get it right." Kuralt, of course, had a story to go with that quote. I don't know how we got on the subject, but we were talking about the dumbest things we ever did.

1 Memo reprinted on www.reuters.com during observance of the 100th anniversary of Paul Julius Reuter's death in 1899.

The dumbest thing I ever did was before I got into television. It was while I was editor of the college paper. I was also the AP [Associated Press] stringer[2] in Chapel Hill, and we had a murder-suicide on campus. I couldn't find out anything on the phone, so I went running over to the hospital to get the story. The young man who had been shot was indeed dead, and a nurse in the hall told me that the other guy, who had shot himself afterward, had also just died. So I filed that to Raleigh and the AP ran it on the "A" wire, nationwide. A murder-suicide in Chapel Hill. The only flaw was that the kid who had shot himself—he did die, but he hadn't died yet when I put that out. The story was out there, and all of a sudden—it makes me short of breath just to think about this—I had a piece of "just torn off the wire" copy handed to me that said, "KILL, KILL. This is a mandatory kill."[3] That was *my* story they were killing, because they found out that the kid wasn't dead, as they had just reported based on my story.

Kuralt called it a mistake of youthful enthusiasm, wanting to get his story on the wire before anybody else. And the lesson he learned, of course, was in plain sight on that very ruler he used to tear stories from the wire machine. "Get it first, but first get it right."

The idea that being right was more important than being first, coupled with the credo set forth by Reuter, gave the wires an almost unchallenged credibility. Borrowing from the old adage "If it's in the paper, it must be true," news editors throughout the world have often been heard to say, "If it's on the wire, it must be true." Such beliefs soon led to the spread of the dread disease known in the industry as "wireitis": a newsroom-borne affliction that causes editors to say, "If it's *not* on the wires, it must *not* be true."

Therein lies an abundance of tales. One of my favorites involves former WCBS Radio newsman Bob Glenn. It seems Glenn had been sent to cover what was a major story in New York at the time. The question was, would innovative Traffic Commissioner Henry Barnes—he's the one who made all the avenues one-way in Manhattan—stay in New York, or

2 Stringer: A freelance (nonstaff) person who submits stories to a news service on a pay-per-story basis. The designation originated when newspapers would pay by the column inch, the length of the column being measured with a piece of string.

3 Mandatory kill: An urgent bulletin sent out by wire services to warn clients not to use a particular story that has just been run, because it is incorrect.

resign his post and return to St. Louis? There were no leaks. No one had even a hint of what his decision would be.

When Glenn arrived at the room where the news conference announcing the decision would be held, he spotted a phone. With a twinkle in his eye, he rushed over and picked it up. Glory be: a dial tone. Glenn quickly dialed the WCBS Radio newsroom and got someone on the writing staff. "Listen," he whispered, "I've gotten hold of a phone in the conference room, and I'm not going to give it up. Write two bulletins—one saying Barnes is staying, the other that he's going. I'll stay on the line and as soon as he announces his decision, I'll tell you which bulletin to take into the studio. We'll beat everybody!"

Glenn spent the next half-hour fending off other reporters who demanded he relinquish the phone to them. He steadfastly refused, telling some that it was in fact his own phone, which WCBS had installed for the occasion. Finally the moment came. The doors to the room closed, the news conference began, and Henry Barnes announced that he was indeed staying in New York. "He's staying," Glenn whispered into the telephone. "Got it?" "Got it," came the response, and Glenn hung up, with visions of the bulletin sounder going on the air as he scooped the entire city press corps.

When Glenn got back to the office, he had a spring in his step and excitement in his voice as he rushed up to his collaborator and asked, "How much did we beat the wires by?"

"We didn't," came the reply.

"What do you mean, we didn't?" Glenn was indignant. "The wire guys were all locked in the room with me. They didn't get out for half an hour after we had the scoop. There's no way they could have beaten us!"

"Well," explained the writer apologetically, "I was running into the studio with the bulletin, just like we planned, when the producer asked me where I was going in such a hurry. I explained it to him, and he told me to 'wait until the wires confirm it.'"

The rest of the conversation is unprintable, even by today's standards.

Not that anyone who was tuned in to WCBS would have been switching stations to see who got the story on air first. That didn't really matter in the scheme of things. It was, however, and remains today a major point of pride in newsrooms. Beat the competition—and, especially, beat the wires.

One of my first jobs in broadcasting was as a copy boy at radio station WMGM in New York. Our newsroom was located about one hundred feet from the studio. The competition was the only other rock 'n' roll station in the city at that time, WINS (home of Top Forty superstar Alan Freed). Their newsroom was also a distance away from their studio. The way we competed was to listen to each other and see whose newsman could rip the bulletin off the wire and run into the studio the fastest. When some of our more portly commentators were on duty, WINS won. We even talked of using roller skates in this battle to "scoop" the competition. We kept score. Of course, the only ones who knew about this mini-war were the news staffs of the two stations. But oh, what fun it was. That is, until one day, when the Associated Press ran a KILL bulletin right after our man had beaten their man down the hall. The cheering in our newsroom as we heard our bulletin sounder on the air was abruptly interrupted by the insistent ringing of the bulletin bells on the teletype machine. We had to go on the air and apologize for the error. It was embarrassing—and after that, our newsmen ran just a little bit slower.

Another carrier of the wireitis virus is the "daybook," a chronological list of events that are taking place on any given day. It tells where and when the event will be, what it's about, and if the wire services will cover it. News editors use this information to decide whether or not to send someone to cover a story.

A reporter at WCBS arrived at the scene of a story one evening only to find the building locked up tight, with absolutely not a soul around. He waited a half-hour past the appointed time and then called the news desk to confirm the address. "There's no one here." "That's ridiculous," countered the editor. "There has to be someone there. It's on the daybook." Well, apparently the people who were supposed to be having the meeting didn't read the daybook, because they failed to show up. The reporter came to that conclusion after hanging around for another half-hour, as ordered. Actually, he came to that conclusion long before he was ordered to hang around, but that's another story.

WHO DO WE THINK WE ARE?

It was the late 1970s and early 1980s. It was a time of turmoil in the ranks of journalism. Journalists were suddenly held in low esteem.

Surveys at the time ranked them below used-car salesmen in terms of trustworthiness. Motives were questioned, and hidden agendas were sought. If Walter Cronkite had been the most trusted man in America, now all journalists were the most *distrusted*: seen as overstepping their bounds at every turn; as arguing and debating with public officials during interviews. CBS's Ed Bradley, for example, was in an argument with a senator on the floor of the Democratic Convention, on live television. CBS took a lot of heat for that.

It was a time networks were getting sued for what some considered overaggressive news coverage. The faked Janet Cooke Pulitzer Prize–winning story brought further disrepute. There were dozens of such incidents in a relatively short period of time. Colleagues lamented that while they were once proud to tell people what they did for a living, they now lied about it rather than face the usual challenge put forth to them at parties and on dates: "Who do you people think you are?"

Longtime ABC radio commentator Paul Harvey gave the issue just that title in a spellbinding speech he gave at a luncheon of the Radio and Television News Directors Association in 1983. Who, indeed, did we think we were? His conclusions notwithstanding, Harvey began his speech with an anecdote that shows just how powerful a wire story can be—how much influence it can wield. This excerpt is from the beginning of his remarks:

> Eighteen ninety-nine: Four newspaper reporters from Denver, Colorado, met by chance on a Saturday night in the Denver rail depot. Al Stephens, Jack Tourney, John Lewis, Hal Wilshire. They represented four Denver papers: the *Post*, the *Times*, the *Republican*, and the *Rocky Mountain News*. Each had been sent by his respective newspaper to dig up a story, any story, for the Sunday edition. So the reporters were at the rail station hoping to snag a visiting celebrity, should one happen to arrive that evening by train. None arrived.
>
> The reporters began commiserating. They were all facing an empty-handed return to their city desks—until Al said, "I'm gonna make up a story. I'm gonna make up something and hand it in." The other three laughed. Someone suggested they go over to the Oxford Hotel across the street and have a beer. They did.

After a beer, Jack said he liked Al's idea about faking a story. "Why not?" A second round of beers. Now a phony domestic story would be too easy to check on, so they began discussing foreign angles, which would be difficult to verify. "China!" China was distant enough, they agreed. They would write about China. And then John leaned forward, gesturing dramatically in the dim light of the barroom. He said, "Let's try this one on. Let's write, um—well, let's say that a . . . a group of American engineers stopped over at the Denver rail station on their way to China. Because the Chinese government—well, let's say the government's making plans to demolish the Great Wall, and our engineers are going over to bid on the job."

Now, Hal was skeptical. Why would the Chinese want to destroy the Great Wall? They all thought about it for a moment, and then one of them decided, "Well, we can say that they're tearing down the ancient boundary to symbolize international good will, as a welcome to foreign trade." Another round of beer.

Now it's eleven p.m. The four reporters have worked out the details of their preposterous story. The Denver newspapers carried the story—all four of them—on the front page. The *Times* headline that Sunday read, "GREAT CHINESE WALL DOOMED: PEKING SEEKS WORLD TRADE." Of course, you know now that that story was a ludicrous fabrication, concocted by four capricious newsmen in a hotel bar. But this is the rest of the story.

It was taken seriously. I mean, it was picked up by newspapers in the Eastern United States. Then by newspapers abroad. And when the Chinese themselves learned that the Americans were sending a demolition crew to tear down their national monument, they were understandably indignant. Some were outraged. Particularly incensed were members of a volatile group of Chinese patriots who were already wary of foreign intervention. Incensed by the story, they rampaged against the foreign embassies in Peking, slaughtering hundreds of missionaries. In two months, twelve thousand troops from six countries joined forces and invaded China to protect their respective interests. It all led to the start of the Boxer Rebellion.

Four newsmen in a bar started a war? Who do we think we are?

Now, I'm taking this story out of context. Paul Harvey used it to show just how far news reporters have gone, and just what impact their musings can have on those who take note of them. I'm using the story in another manner. Consider this (and I am speculating here): No doubt the wire services, such as they were—the news agencies that picked up news from here and passed it on to there—carried those stories that originated at that Denver bar in the minds of those four reporters. And no doubt, no editor, from the *New York Times* to the *London Times* and all the newspapers in between, who carried that story—no doubt no editor questioned that story or hesitated to use it. Why? Because it was on the wire!

Now, it's January 20, 1981. We stood mesmerized in a tense newsroom at CBS—all eyes on four television sets, soundlessly showing us some of the most dramatic images of the decade. There was Jimmy Carter, outgoing president of the United States, pacing the Oval Office, his eyes on a television picture. There was Ronald Reagan, about to be sworn in as the fortieth president of the United States. The ceremony was to begin now. It was noon. Yet both men waited. Both intently watched a television picture beamed by satellite from across the globe. It was an image of an airliner sitting on the tarmac of Teheran airport. The plane was surrounded by Iranian troops. On board were fifty-two Americans, taken hostage 444 days before at the American embassy in Teheran and about to be released. You could see the wavy lines of heat rising from the black runway. You could see the anxiety in the faces of the two great world leaders whose fates were intertwined with what was playing out on television. The plane had been scheduled to take off for freedom at noon. It was almost a minute past, and there was no sign of movement by the troops or the plane. There was no sign that the transfer of presidential power would take place until that plane took off. The tension was palpable.

Just then, startling those of us standing near the wire service machine room, five bells rang out. It was Reuters. They moved a "snap," which is the highest-priority bulletin. We rushed in and grabbed it. It said that the plane containing the fifty-two American hostages had taken off from Iran and was headed to Wiesbaden, Germany. We looked up at the television screen. The plane still sat there. The wavy lines of intense heat still rose before the camera. The soldiers were still in place. The presidents, one soon to leave office and one soon to begin his term, were still waiting.

Mutual Radio, I guess, didn't have their TV on, because—so the story goes—a news manager there grabbed the snap bulletin from the wire machine, dashed into the studio where the noon newscast was in progress, pushed the newscaster aside, and announced to the world that Mutual News had learned that the plane had taken off.

After all, it was on the wire.

9

TO ACT OR NOT TO ACT: THAT IS THE DEBATE

My knees weakened as I pushed through the revolving door under the Art Deco marquee that shouted "NBC STUDIOS" in red neon. I was 26 years old, in the radio news business for several years, and heading for the big time. At least, I hoped I was. No, I was certain of it. It was my dream come true, an audition at NBC Radio News. As I entered the building and took the chrome-and-brass elevators to the second floor, I gasped as I saw the huge windows that looked into the radio studios I had seen so many times before. I remembered sneaking out of grade school early, taking the subway to Rockefeller Center with my friend Bob Balfour. We would sit in the front row of the audience at the *Bob and Ray Show*, which was broadcast live every day at 4:00 p.m. from deep within the labyrinth of NBC. Then we would slip into one of the guided tours as it snaked through the endless corridors. Dozens of times we saw the sound effects rooms, the studios where live programs were broadcast, the early TV facilities. I remembered the huge cameras; the massive lights; and the kinescope rooms, where live TV shows were being filmed for the record. (Videotape had yet to be invented.)

What I remembered most, however, was looking longingly into the giant, twin radio studios on the second floor—the ones from which *Monitor Radio* was broadcast over the network every weekend. I remembered looking at the clocks hung across the back wall, each show-ing the time in another part of the world, and, below them, the giant windows that separated the studios from the control room. I remem-bered picturing myself in there broadcasting the news, saying, "This is Art Athens for NBC News."

Now, all these years later, I still felt the thrill I had as that eighth-grade kid. I'd already been a news guy for eight years, having started on the air right out of high school. I was working at the time as news director at a suburban radio station. I loved my job. It was at an Associated Press awards ceremony that I met Tony DeHaro, who was running NBC Radio News. I was there to accept a number of honors. He seemed impressed. "Come on down," he had told me. "We'll be glad to give you a shot at a job at NBC." This was it. My chance of a lifetime. My shot at the big time!

So here I was. I arrived at the NBC studios and, using the deepest voice I could muster, I asked for DeHaro. I told him I was ready for the challenge. He gave me some material from the wire services and asked me to write a five-minute newscast. That was easy for me; I was always a quick and confident writer. Half an hour later, my voice in its lowest reg-ister, I brought DeHaro my news copy and boomed, "All set, Mr. DeHaro." As I recall now, I think I forced my voice so low that I actual-ly hurt myself. But I knew I sounded great, just like those NBC guys.

He looked over the copy, said it was fine, and told me to follow him. Wouldn't you know it? We went right into the giant studios I had always gawked at through the glass while on those stolen tours. My legs turned rubbery—I couldn't believe it. He sat me down at the table, facing all those clocks and the massive control room window. He left me there, with a big microphone hanging in front of my face, a microphone that had probably been used by Ken Banghart, Chet Huntley, perhaps even Bob and Ray. I swallowed hard. DeHaro told me to put on the headphones, and he went into the control room. I heard his voice tell me to read the news opening from the format sheet lying on the table, so they could get a sound level. In my deepest baritone voice I said, "NBC News on the hour. I'm Art Athens, and at this hour . . ." I stopped. He said, "That's fine. In a few seconds you will hear the NBC News opening theme, they will point to you, and you can begin." "OK," I said. Wow. This was it, my future on the line right here and right now.

Just then, a guided tour glided up outside the big window, the same tour and the same window that had thrilled me so much as a kid. They were all looking at me. The tour guide was talking to them and pointing at me. At *me*! My stomach knotted. The NBC News theme crackled through my earphones. The finger pointed, and I said, "NBC News on the hour. I'm Art Athens, and at this hour . . ." This time I didn't stop; I went ahead and read the newscast I had written. There was just one problem. I was so nervous, my voice cracked with the very first syllable I spoke, and I sounded like a cross between Michael Jackson and Tiny Tim. I felt my head pound and my knees shake, and when it was all over I knew I had blown my one and only chance in a lifetime to make the big time. My life was over. I would never reach my goal. It was time to pack it in. Find a new career. Maybe leave the country. Obviously, I didn't get the job.

Now there is a very important point to this story. I was convinced my career as a news broadcaster was over, and it was really all I had ever wanted to do. In a last, desperate attempt to save my life's ambition, I decided that what I needed was voice lessons. I could write well; I knew that. I knew I could cover a story better than anybody. What I couldn't do was *sound* good enough. As soon as I left NBC I looked in the *New York Times*. There were dozens of classified ads for people giving voice, singing, and acting lessons. I picked one at random, called and explained my problem, and made an appointment for the following week. "Bring some news copy with you when you come," advised the man on the other end. So I did.

I don't remember exactly where it was, but the small studio was in a walk-up building in the forties, off Broadway. It was in the heart of the theater district, in a building like so many that housed rehearsal halls and dance studios. You could hear the cacophony of music and scales as you walked down the dimly lit hallways, just as you can smell the mélange of odors from the many kitchens on an apartment-house floor when you get off the elevator. I remember the guy was dressed in the "beatnik" style popular back then: loose-fitting old sweatshirt, torn jeans, no socks, sandals. He was warm and reassuring as I entered, and we got right down to business. I explained that I wanted more than anything to be a newscaster in the big time. "Alright," he said, "read me some news." I started reading the material I had brought along, and I didn't even get through the first story when he stopped me.

"That's enough," he said gently. "I think I know what your problem is." Already? Wow. This guy's good. What could it be? Diction? Breathing? Inflection? "You don't need *voice* lessons at all," he said matter-of-factly. "What you need is *acting* lessons!"

"Hold it right there," I insisted. I was prepared to ward off the sales pitch I knew was about to befall me. "I'm not interested in any *acting* lessons at all!" I said, growing more determined. "All I want is to be a newscaster. *Period*! Not an actor." I was still a little angry at the apparent bait-and-switch sales routine he was trying to pull on me when he exclaimed, "You don't understand. What I'm telling you is that you are not reading me the news the way *Art Athens* would read me the news. You're reading me the news the way you *think* a newscaster should sound when reading the news. You are probably trying to sound like a composite of newscasters you've heard and admired. In other words, instead of being *yourself*, you are *acting*!"

Well, you could have knocked me over with a feather, along with all those other newscasters I was pretending to be. I got it right away. I took his advice to heart, asked what I owed him, and he said, "Nothing." Just like that. He changed my life forever, and I can't even remember his name. But I remember his lesson, and I have passed it on a hundred times and more. Be yourself. Don't act.

"Now," as Paul Harvey would say, "the rest of the story."

The Osgood Files

As always, Charles Osgood has a good story to tell. This one is about the very first television broadcast he ever did.

I had been working at CBS Radio for a little while. [CBS news president] Dick Salant had said he wanted me to do some television too, and I did some pieces for television, but I felt awkward and I didn't feel as if I were very good. I thought radio was really what I was more interested in and what I wanted to do. But this was CBS News; you couldn't very well not do television. So I was out in California doing some piece, and I got a call from [CBS News executive] Gordon Manning. He said, "Roger Mudd is going to be off and I'd like you to do the *Evening News* Saturday night." "What do you mean, do the

Evening News?" He said, "Anchor the *Evening News.*"

I'd never done a local newscast, never so much as one, ever. I had no idea what it was like or what to do. So I'm petrified, absolutely petrified. I go in there and . . . they're making me up. Nobody has ever made me up before. I'm sitting there and the lights are very bright, and they're coming in and they're telling me things and putting things down I'm supposed to be looking at. I had written some copy, but I'd never written on a TelePrompTer machine before; I used typewriters at WCBS Radio when I was there. I was petrified, and I was also terrible. Opening night was pretty bad.

In those days, they used to open the newscast with what they call a clicker. "From our newsroom in New York, the CBS Evening News with ⸻," and then they would say, "with Walter Cronkite" if it was in the middle of the week or "with Roger Mudd" or whoever it was, and then the clicker, which was the datelines of the stories and then a little dotted line going across the screen and the correspondent who was covering the story. And they did the lineup in front of the picture of the anchorman, a sort of profile picture of him, and he was there, waiting to go on. And then they said, "And now here is Charles Osgood." And the camera comes on and you say, "Good evening, blah, blah, blah . . ."

When I got off the air this particular night I knew I was terrible, because I knew I was frightened. My mouth was dry . . . I was so self-conscious—I was terrible. I was trying to focus on what I was saying, but I couldn't do it. And as soon as I got off the air, there was a telephone call.

"Mike Wallace wants to talk to you." So he said, "Osgood, Monday morning, nine o'clock, I want you in my office with a tape of that show I just saw. Bring it in—Let's go over it. You need a lot of help," he said. I said, "I certainly do need a lot of help." I felt bad about the way it had gone, but I felt worse that Mike Wallace himself had seen this and felt that, as an act of mercy, he needed to intervene.

So I brought the tape in and they put the thing on, and the announcer comes on and the clicker starts and Wallace said, "Look, you're sitting there and you look as if you're about to be executed. You look exactly like a man sitting in an electric chair, waiting for them to pull the switch."

"Stop the tape!" he said. "Walter Cronkite would kill me for saying this. Dick Salant would kill me for saying this, but there's something you have to understand. This is an *acting* job. What we do on television is an acting job, and I'm not going to give you any ten-cent Stanislavsky, but I'll tell you this much: that even before you opened your mouth, I knew that this was going to be *bad*. And the reason that I knew you were going to be bad is because if you are playing the part of an anchorman for CBS News, sitting in Walter Cronkite's chair, doing the news, somebody must have thought that you were able to do that or they wouldn't have put you there. You look as if you snuck into the room in the middle of the night; went around and sat in Walter Cronkite's chair, sort of like . . . , 'Oh, I don't want anyone to see me here;' and you're just waiting for somebody to catch you sitting in Walter Cronkite's chair."

He continued, "Now, if you're an actor, you're playing this role. That's not a desk; that's *your* desk. That's not a chair; that's *your* chair. This copy that's there, these people that are sitting around; they're working for *you*. You're playing the part of somebody who is a *big shot*. So you have to play it that way. If you're playing the part of the big boss, you can't look as though you're afraid of your shadow."

He said, "What they teach you in acting class is, OK, they teach you how to walk. Everyone knows how to walk, but an actor has to . . . there has to be a certain purpose to it. If you're sitting down in a chair, the way you sit down in the chair tells the audience something. It's 'I'm sitting down, and I've had a hard, long day. Whew. I finally get to sit down.' Or, 'I'm going to sit in this chair, and that guy's going to come in and I'm going to fire him!' Or, 'I've got a lot a work to do, I'm a busy man here, I've got a lot of stuff to do, let me get started.' The way you sit communicates all that. That's before you even open your mouth. Then, of course, when you open your mouth it becomes ten times worse, because of your inflection, the pitch of your voice, the look on your face, the eyes when you're talking to the audience." I think that was a very interesting admission on his part, that this is an acting job.

I asked Osgood if he agreed with everything Wallace told him. "Yeah, I do."

I asked, "Does that take away from the journalist part of it? Does it demean that?" "Yeah," said Charlie, "some people would say, of course it does. That's why you can never admit that it's an acting job."

Mike Wallace is certainly willing to admit that it's an acting job of sorts. "We wince when we call ourselves performers. We wince when other people call us performers. But the fact of the matter is, you're a performer. Certainly in broadcast journalism, whether it's radio or television."

This whole topic—Charlie's story, my own experience—led to this conversation with Mike.

ATHENS: A thread seems to be running through all of this, almost two conflicting things: 1) Be yourself; and 2) the advice you gave Osgood—act!

WALLACE: The acting . . . when I started at Grand Rapids, for instance, I'll never forget, on the networks at the time, they had the *Pot of Gold*, which was a kind of game show. So they did a copy of it called the *Sack of Silver* on WOOD in Grand Rapids. This had nothing to do with news. They chose me to do it. And what would happen was that we'd go through telephone books and eventually somebody would choose a number and I would call them on the phone, and if they answered, they would get twenty dollars. And I remember distinctly, on one occasion, I called and said, "This is Myron Wallace and you've won twenty dollars," and the lady at the other end was crying, and I said, I totally forgot [I was on the air] and I said, "What's going on? Why are you crying?" and she said, "I lost . . . I just lost my husband." And I said, "Oh, no. Jesus Christ, what a shame." Live, on the air. This is in Grand Rapids, Dutch Reformed. I was off for the next couple of days, and the people of Grand Rapids heard the story of what had happened and they thought that 'cause I was off the air, I had lost my job for having said that. And so there were all kinds of telephone calls and letters and so forth, and there were a couple of articles in the *Grand Rapids Press*, and I kept my job. It's another thing . . . it's a business of communicating with . . . of reaching the people that you're talking to.

Wallace realized that to really reach people, you had to cross the line of staid and detached behavior. While his reaction to the woman's reply was natural and spontaneous, it was also dramatic—poignant in its way. It got peoples' attention. It moved them to write and call. It was noticed, and Mike noticed that it was noticed. All of his radio activities, which at that time included acting in radio dramas, doing talk and entertainment shows, and even announcing on the *Lone Ranger* broadcast, taught him that there was a special way to communicate effectively with an audience that went beyond just reading the words on a paper.

ATHENS: Does that not, though—I'll ask this as the devil's advocate—does that not undermine your substance? Your credibility?

WALLACE: No. It *could*. But when I say "performer," I mean if you're a writer, you've got a style. Somebody is a pedestrian writer, he gets the facts right, but you don't necessarily want to read what he has to say. Well, the same thing is true on radio and television, as far as news is concerned. You're covering the substance of the news, but if you can make it interesting . . . There's a fellow down the hall here by the name of Ed Bradley. He takes command of that tube. You want to hear what he has to say, and the same thing is true with Morley [Safer]. I mean, there are certain people who simply take charge of the tube. You become a character. You have your style. And to that degree, performance is what it is. That doesn't necessarily impinge upon the substance of your report. You're still doing who, what, when, where, why. You're still telling the facts, but you're telling them in an interesting and compelling fashion.

ATHENS: Someone asked me once, "What kind of an interviewer are you?" I said, "I'm whatever kind of an interviewer I need to be to get the kind of interview I want. I can be tough, I can be naïve, I can be funny, I can be friendly, I can be . . . whatever." You are the dean of interviewers. And [referring to a recent interview in *Playboy* magazine] you got into this whole discussion about acting . . . I don't think the guy got it.

WALLACE: I think he got it, and maybe I just didn't express it sufficiently. I mean, he kept, in a sense, asking me the same question, "How can you be a performer and a reporter at the same time?" Well, you can be. Are you telling me that Peter Jennings and Tom Brokaw and Dan Rather are not performers? They're first-class newsmen, but the reason that they are in the jobs that they are in is because they can capture the audience's attention and hold the audience's attention—by manner, by speech, by the way they take command of the tube.

ATHENS: But . . . I'm just trying to marry, and maybe I can't . . . to marry the two concepts of 1) perform in such a way as to best communicate whatever it is you're trying to communicate, because that's your ultimate goal; and 2) be yourself; don't be contrived. And so you have to have a certain natural feel for it.

WALLACE: Yes, but what happens . . . if you do it long enough, over and over and over again, and you know who you are . . . you can't do this in a week. You can't learn to do this in a year, necessarily. You need the opportunity to do it over and over and over, and find out what works and find out what doesn't work, and find out about all of the techniques that are involved in communicating with an audience, which is, after all, the object. If you're a print reporter . . . I'll pick up the paper: When I see Tom Friedman, for instance, on the *New York Times* Op-Ed page, I want to read it. I want to read Maureen Dowd. I want to read Anthony Lewis. I want to read Bill Safire. I get substance from them, but they have their own interesting, compelling style. The same thing is true in television. People who want to watch me—you know, they endow me with the business that I'm a digger, that I'm willing to ask the irreverent or abrasive question. Fine, fine, because that means they'll pay attention. And over a period of time, if you don't let them down, if your reports are accurate and fair, and you're asking the questions in interviews that are on the audience's mind, you're a surrogate for them. To me, that does not diminish the integrity of the job; it just means that you're doing it in a more interesting and more compelling way.

President Ronald Reagan was known as "the great communicator." In the words of Brian Williams, "It's Ronald Reagan's gift. Ronald Reagan knew the punchy phrase. He knew facial technique. He knew when and where to look, and he did it better than any modern, media-era president."

Ronald Reagan was, of course, an actor. I asked Williams if when it comes to television we should start thinking about that little facial move: where to look, when to look there, or how to glance at our coanchor or the camera at a particular moment. Would that be as important as what we have to say? Williams replied,

No, well because . . . speaking for myself, I've never put on a move or a look in my life. I treat the camera like it's my wife. Someone told me long ago: You're having a conversation. Picture a focus group of your closest friends: an old family friend from Pennsylvania, your wife, your parents, friends from school, your parents' friends, older folks who may have a hard time hearing and you have to enunciate. Picture a group, a warm and friendly group of eyes listening to you. That's whom you're communicating with. That's whom I've always been communicating with. I never give that camera a look or a glance that I wouldn't give my wife at the dinner table. I've never had a pre-ordained move in my life on camera.

I have worked next to an anchor who has put expressions and what to do in parentheses, in the margin. My last day at a certain television station, the word "kiss" was in the margin when she turned to kiss me and wish me well on the air. And I worked with an anchor in Kansas who wrote "smile" at certain moments and "serious" at others, next to her script. These are people without the natural ability to do a quick summation of the very words—God knows they didn't write them—but of the very words they are reading off the TelePrompTer. They have no connection with the English language. They have no feeling. They don't know from human emotions, so they have to instruct themselves.

Someone who rarely showed emotion on the air was Walter Cronkite.

ATHENS: Let's talk a little about on-air persona. I can ask ten people and get ten different answers. The question of performance: Brian Williams says, "Never," and Mike Wallace says, "Always." Is it a performance?

CRONKITE: Well, I say never, although I will admit that those who perform, particularly in the case of Mike Wallace, do it very well. But to me, I never tried to perform. If it appeared that I was performing, it was certainly accidental.

ATHENS: Now when you cried at the Kennedy funeral, or when you were choked up at the moon shot . . .

CRONKITE: That certainly was no performance. I was embarrassed at having been nearly speechless for a moment. I was embarrassed about that. I was later very pleased when the new gentility vogue set in for males, and we were permitted to have emotions and to cry occasionally, because I do on occasion. I mostly cry over the death of animals; but anyway, I'm not ashamed. I'm not ashamed of my emotions, but I certainly . . . I would be very ashamed if I faked them.

ATHENS: Well, that's what I was going to ask you. I've heard stories of anchors who have notations on the TelePrompTer that say, "Look sad here," or "Laugh here."

CRONKITE: I've seen them on the air, and I can almost see that there's somebody prompting them, or they prompt themselves to do something like that. I'm sorry that that's the case. I don't think it has done any good for our business. It may be part of the reason that today there's so much of a kind of dissatisfaction, I think, from the public regarding our on-air performance.

ATHENS: Going back to what I mentioned earlier, a litmus test: If someone has to be told when to be sad or happy or to smile, maybe they should be selling insurance instead of selling information?

CRONKITE: Of course they should be. In fact, I wouldn't want them selling me insurance, either. I don't want them being sad about my future, or the fact that I'm likely to konk off at any moment. That's not what I want. I want somebody to just put the facts in front of me. I think some of us have a great suspicion about emotionalism, as such. I can be very emotional. I can be emotional about a superb performance on the stage. I see somebody just doing what they're supposed to do so magnificently, I'll get tears in my eyes, just watching that performance. So it's not that I abhor emoting when emoting is called for, but I don't think it's called for in news broadcasting.

In fact, Walter Cronkite had a very definite idea of what he thought news broadcasting should be all about, and he had it early in his career at CBS. Charles Osgood tells a tale-out-of-school that relates directly to all this acting business.

OSGOOD: Walter had a reputation for being a life-of-the-party kind of guy. He would have people over every year for a Christmas party, and the highlight of the party was always Walter's hoochie-coochie dance, where he would do bumps and grinds. Walter Cronkite! Great raconteur, wonderful storyteller, and all that. And somebody had the idea when they decided to do a morning news show to run opposite the *Today Show*, they knew just who to get—they'd get Walter Cronkite. At that point, Doug Edwards was still doing the evening news. Everybody who knew Walter figured that this was going to be just great, because Walter was a real person and would come across real. Not only that, but he was funny and had a lot of stories and he'd be just great. So lo and behold, they stuck him on there. In fact, they even put him on there with a puppet, a lion by the name of Charlemagne, because that's the kind of thing they wanted: "It's Walter Cronkite and Charlemagne, the puppet." But Walter, from the day that he started the show, would say [imitates a very serious Cronkite], "Good morning. I'm Walter Cronkite and this is the news this morning." On television, doing the news, he was not about to slip into that other persona.

ATHENS: The hoochie-coochie mode.

OSGOOD: No. Because he had a sense, which I think is a very valuable sense, of how a person doing that should be. And he never lost that sense, and he got better at it as he went along. He defined it himself; he didn't have somebody say, "Here's what I want. Give me a little more friendly, give me a little more smile here . . ." I've got a friend who drives me crazy. Back when I was first trying to do the news on television and he was trying to help me, he'd say, "The lines in your forehead need to go . . . we need to be able to see these lines here. When you do like this . . . and the lines go like that . . . then that's not likable. You want to be with someone who's friendly, and that means like that: eyebrows up, lines going like that . . ." But I mean, Walter would never listen to that for a second. I mean, I hated that.

Dan Rather succeeded Cronkite to that coveted CBS anchor chair. I told Dan about Mike Wallace's advice to Osgood, and about how Brian Williams told me he talks to the camera just as he would talk to his wife across the kitchen table. Dan smiled at that.

First of all, I respect Brian tremendously, but I point out to you that this is where a journalist's skepticism might come in. I believe that Brian wants to believe that himself, and he wants to have the audience believe that. I do have some doubt, with all respect, that that is in fact the way he talks to his wife across the kitchen table. Because, you see, if it is, I feel sorry for his wife. I know Brian very well. I think I know what he's talking about. I don't mean to be critical—he's a great young pro, and I think he's terrific. He's a really good pro.

But . . . Mike [Wallace] and I had this conversation. I have a different view. When Mike Wallace speaks, I listen and I listen closely, because there's nobody in the business that I respect more. But about this, honest people can differ, and they do differ, person-to-person, profession-to-profession. I took Mike's advice a long time ago; I tried it. It didn't work. It still doesn't work. I do not come to the set viewing myself as a performer. I do not come to the *CBS Evening News* viewing it as a performance. Even though I had the great Mike Wallace's counsel ringing in my ears, it didn't work for me. I have no doubt that it works for Mike. It may very well work for Charlie Osgood, another good friend of mine. It doesn't work for me.

What does work for me, and it took me a while to come to this, is a version of . . . "I am what I am." It's a mistake to try to be anything else. What I am is a reporter. That's what I am. That's what I've dedicated my life to, my professional life. That's my passion. Television is not my passion; *the news* is my passion. And it has to do with one's gift. Mine is news. What is it about? News! What am *I* about? News! What's in my heart? News! When I step up there tonight, my goal is to appear to be what I am. This guy's a reporter. He isn't a performer. I'm fond of saying, "I'm a reporter. I don't just play one on TV." I think there is a trap to putting too much emphasis on performing. To paraphrase Martin Luther, "This is where I stand . . . I can stand in no other place."

The news is there to report and to write, and then you think what is the best way, what is the clearest, most understandable way to communicate to the viewer what I know as a reporter and what I've written. Now, when I talk to the camera, I do try to talk one-on-one, and I think this is what Brian's doing, too. And I've said for years, this is the way I was taught about television. It has worked for me and I believe it, and that is, when you look down that barrel into the camera lens, that's what you do: You think of your mother, think of your girlfriend, think of your wife, and talk to them. Talk—don't announce. That is truth that works for me. I have been at my worst when I've tried to think of myself as a performer, and of what I do on television as a performance. Perhaps Mike's way works for some people. It does-n't work for me.

Rather remembers the time he did try using the Wallace method. He had been a reporter with CBS for a number of years, and then his big chance came: a shot at anchoring the Sunday-night network news. It was a big deal.

So I got what amounted to a tryout, and it was at that time that I tried Mike's advice, what I'd heard him say, which you described ear-lier. And I came to it saying, "OK, I'd better think of this as a perform-ance. I've got to think of myself as a performer." I had not done that in Houston [earlier in his career]. But this was the big time. These were the big leagues. If the great Mike Wallace says that this is the way to do it . . ."

Rather sat in that Sunday anchor chair in an audition that lasted sev-eral weeks.

I was uncomfortable within myself, but I tried for a number of weeks, and the decision maker at the time said a version of, "I have to tell you that this doesn't look like the right thing for you." He said, "I think you're very good. You can be a great reporter, terrific field reporter for television, but I don't think you're cutting it this way." That's when I said to myself, "Well, if I'm going to go down, I'm going down being myself. If this is my last day at anchoring, I'm at least going to give people a look at who I am and what I am.

Dan Rather did what he thought was his last anchoring newscast without performing. He was just himself. Not wanting this to sound like a fairy-tale ending, but the man who made the decisions said, "Well, I still don't think you're terrific, but I do see something . . ." And Dan Rather kept his Sunday-night anchor job.

So does that prove Mike Wallace is wrong about having to perform?

Well, nobody was more natural and "himself" than Charles Kuralt. Being real was his credo.

Yeah, I mean that is practical career advice, I think, because it will be apparent to people that you're earnest and just trying to tell a story. Think about the best reporters you've ever known. Almost all of them are just so consumed by the story they're telling that they sort of forget about . . . I used to get irritated with Izzy [his cameraman]. He would say, "Comb your hair," or, "You've got dandruff on your . . ." And I'd say, "It doesn't matter, let's . . . don't interrupt."

So then, what about this acting business?

Well, acting was all the style when I started. I mean . . . everything I've just said did not apply; it did not apply to the reporters of the fifties, who *were* the story, in a sense. I mean, [Edward R.] Murrow certainly worried about his appearance and certainly chose his on-camera words and appearance very carefully.

There's a story about Murrow and his famous World War II broadcasts from the roofs of London during Nazi air raids. Murrow would begin each broadcast with the sounds of planes and antiaircraft fire in the background and the words "This is London." These live broadcasts from overseas were an amazing feat in those days. Millions of Americans would sit spellbound by their radios—remember, this was before TV—as Murrow and CBS brought the war in Europe into homes across America. Now Murrow kept in touch with and was very influenced by an old high school English teacher. After she heard Murrow's live broadcast and his words "This is London," so the story goes, she contacted him. She suggested he put a dramatic pause between his opening words, to add impact and emphasis to what he was saying and from where he was saying it. Murrow took that advice, and henceforth, he opened many of his CBS broadcasts, "*This* . . . is London."

Now, back to Charles Kuralt and our discussion of acting.

What we were talking about was acting, and they were all actors. I mean [CBS News correspondent Charles] Collingwood and the rest of them were. All but [Eric] Severeid. I mean, I think the writing was a lot better then. They were scholar-journalists in a way that hardly anybody is today. I think of Tom Fenton at CBS and maybe

Bruce Morton, who's gone over to CNN now, and a handful of others; but all of those guys were great specialists and thinkers and writers and actors. Severeid hated that part of it. You know, "One good word is worth a thousand pictures" is the famous remark that he made. And he never was comfortable with the lights and the cameras and all of that stuff. Handsome as he was, and, I think, as good a reader of his own stuff as he was, he never became comfortable with it.

I abandoned—maybe not completely, but I certainly diminished my acting as my life went on. When I look back at some of those early stories I did in the fifties and early sixties, I'm consciously trying to sound like Murrow, the way so many young reporters over at NBC consciously tried to sound like David Brinkley for years. They developed his intonations and all. Well, they're both good choices, but better to just be yourself. I've had occasion to look back at some of those very early stories I did in black-and-white film and all that, and I see that I was far too formal. As the years went by I learned to just be more conversational and say things on television the way I would if I were just talking to one person. It's not a multitude you're talking to; it's just that one guy watching his TV set at home.

Well, maybe Mike Wallace is right about this. I mean, all those old-timers, the groundbreakers in broadcast news, the icons of the industry—they were performing well as well as writing well.

But then, maybe it's just plain, good old communication skills. Let's give Andy Rooney the last word on that.

I don't know, I suppose it is. Years ago I was doing an hour documentary about Washington, *Mr. Rooney Goes to Washington.* I'm sitting at my desk telling the story about how a bureaucrat has a lot of jobs available and he has an old college roommate who needs a job, so he rewrites the job description to fit his roommate before he calls him in. Anyway, I'm telling the story, and I say, "Say my old college roommate comes into my office," and I lean back and then I tell the story. Then my cameraman, Walter, says, "Geez Andy, that was so great," and he says, "It looked so natural when you leaned back that way. Except I wasn't expecting it. I just lost the top of your head. Do it once more, just the way you did it." And I thought, "Oh, Jesus, I'll have an acting career in twenty years."

"And you did it?"
"No, I didn't. I said, you're going have to go with what you have."

All the world's a stage. Or is it?

*" It is better to ask some of the questions
than to know all of the answers. "*
JAMES THURBER

10

How Can They *Ask* That?
~QUESTIONING THE QUESTIONERS~

In the early 1940s, Edward R. Murrow brought the war in Europe to life in American homes with well-chosen words on the radio. In the mid-1960s, television brought the bloody battlegrounds of the Vietnam War into our living rooms on film and tape. It was graphic reality. Then, in the early 1990s, the coverage of the Persian Gulf War invaded our sensibilities as well as our homes, making for an experience that can only be described as surreal. It was the latter part of 1990, at the height of the Persian Gulf War, dubbed Desert Storm. Sitting in front of our sets, we watched the bombing of Beirut by the United States from the vantage point of a correspondent's hotel room window. *Live,* as it happened.

We watched a handsome young NBC correspondent—they called him the Scud Stud—literally duck to avoid being hit by Scud missiles fired by Iraq at U.S. military bases in Egypt as he broadcast from a rooftop. *Live,* as it happened. We could watch the war we were waging in real time, as it actually unfolded. So could the enemy—on CNN, broadcast live, around the world.

But the most amazing part of it all was the news conference routine we would all go through every day. *Live,* as it happened. It made U.S. generals like "Stormin'" Norman Schwartzkopf and Colin Powell into cult figures. And the questions asked at those press conferences—Oh, the questions! Questions so absurd, they inspired a *Saturday Night Live* skit duplicating an on-air Q&A with dead-on accuracy. I cringe, even today, at the tone and temper of the questions these overanxious, obnoxious, uninformed so-called journalists would ask. Each one was figuring to pick up a Pulitzer Prize or two for breaking the big story about the United States's secret plans to win the war. At least that's how it came out in my mind.

I cannot remember exactly what the questions posed to *SNL*'s "Schwartzkopf" and "Powell" were, but I can remember the tone. It went something like this.

+ What time will the surprise attack begin?

+ How many troops will we use for the invasion, and where are they hiding?

+ Will we send in our aircraft from the North? How many planes? At what time?

Hilarious . . . but not one bit funny.

Why did they ask such questions? These reporters were not thinking at all. We've all seen reporters who go up to the parents whose child has been killed and ask, "How do you feel, having lost your only child in this plane crash?" It happens all the time. You know it does. What answer do they expect? Perhaps something like, "Oh, we're glad he's dead. He was always a pain in the ass to take care of, and besides, we had him heavily insured and we can use the money"?

The sad truth is that many reporters *are* thinking; but what they're thinking is that they want to distinguish themselves as quickly as possible so they can be as famous as Dan Rather or Tom Brokaw or Mike Wallace or Ed Bradley. I think they truly believe that their question ("What time will the sneak attack take place, and where will it be?") is the one that's going to catapult them into the big time. But Rather and Brokaw and Wallace and Bradley didn't get where they are by asking stupid questions or having delusions of grandeur. As Ed Bradley notes, one of the most important parts of asking is *listening*. "Just listen, *listen*. You ask a question—listen to what the person says to you. You ask a question. You've got a follow-up question. Well, maybe what they said takes you in another direction. You have to listen to that to see which way to go with it."

The problem is, most reporters and interviewers get so wrapped up in thinking about what they're going to ask next, they don't listen to the answers to what they've already asked. Sometimes they ask questions without even realizing that the interviewee has just given them the information they are asking about. I recall watching just such an interview by a so-called world-class interviewer who was questioning American playwright, legislator, and diplomat Clare Boothe Luce as they sat on the patio of her home in Hawaii. It was the start of the interview, and he had asked her how she liked living in Hawaii. She gushed about how it had been the best five years of their lives, that since giving up living in Washington five years before, she and her husband, publisher Henry Luce, had really learned to love Hawaii, and that they hoped to spend many more years there that were just as rewarding as those first five had been.

"How long have you been living here?" asked the interviewer. He was serious. I was on the floor laughing. The classy Mrs. Luce simply replied, "Five years."

The Story of "Oh"

It doesn't really matter whom you are interviewing or what the topic is: The best way to get information from someone is to just let it come out naturally. I don't know about you, but I can't stand the interviewer who simply won't allow a nanosecond of silence at the end of a sentence. As soon as the interview subject stops for a breath, the next question is flying though the air at the speed of light. One of the most effective questions I've ever asked is a tiny, lonely little word: "Oh?"

For example, someone would say, "I never did like the way they ran that place." And I would say, "Oh?" Then I'd wait. Pretty soon, the person I was interviewing would figure out that she was supposed to say something. So then she would fill in the silence with, perhaps, *why* the place wasn't run well, or who didn't run it well, or what happened to make her feel that way. It's a very powerful little question, that "Oh?" The key is: To make it work, the questioner must follow it with silence.

Mike Wallace is probably the undisputed toughest news interviewer on the face of the earth. He is known for his direct, irreverent, often withering questions. Wallace says that while research and preparation are important, *listening* is the most important element of all.

Some interviewers listen to answers and all they want to do is, "OK, you say that John killed Jack? OK." And then they go on to their next question. I mean if you *listen*, and you really listen, the questions come one after the other after the other. Frequently, all you've got to ask is, "Because? Because? Why?" I have found so many people whom I've interviewed, who will make a statement that I don't fully understand, or the audience doesn't fully understand. So I say, "Because?" and they explain it to you. And then they get caught up and . . . look, you and I are looking at each other now. There is eye contact. You're listening to me and I'm listening to you. And if a camera were over there, all of a sudden you forget the camera, you forget the lights. There are just two people locked in conversation. That used to be such fun back in the old days of *Night Beat*[1] on Channel 5. The interview subject was in a chair and I was on a stool, and I had my questions and I had my cigarette, and it was dark and all of that. Suddenly, you realized, you've locked on to each other and you can forget everything else in the studio. We're just going back and forth, and that's one of the most satisfying things you can do.

The interview, in other words, suddenly becomes a conversation. Instead of trying to get through a list of questions in hand, a good interviewer actually tries to learn something from the interview subject by listening. By being curious. By letting the story unfold, instead of trying to steer it to a preconceived place.

Jerry Nachman, a CBS colleague for many years, was a great interviewer. More than that, he was an *observer*, which is really what a good reporter needs to be. He agrees that listening is an important form of observation and interviewing.

1 Night Beat: a breakthrough 1950s tough one-on-one interview show in which Wallace would interrogate guests willing to sit in the so-called hot seat. It was dramatically broadcast against a black background on the old Dumont station in New York. It made Wallace's reputation as a tough interviewer.

The biggest problem in questioning is not listening. You see this on TV all the time. A person has a list of questions, and they have no idea what the other person said—because they're either thinking of their next ad-lib or they're going to the next question. And I've laughed about this all my life. Curt Clemmens [a NYC radio reporter] had the best question I ever heard. He had only one question. He asked it on every story, every time, every day, and it was the best question in the history of journalism. He said, "What are we standing in front of this-here building for?" That's the best question I've ever heard. [Mocking a political candidate:] "I come here today to announce my candidacy . . . I'm here today to say that I will be vindicated in this . . ." It was great. He had no idea who he was covering or why, but he said, "What are we standing in front of this-here building for?"

My favorite question was, "What the fuck does that *mean?*" You remember that? I used to ask that at Channel 2 all the time . . . on tape. "What the fuck does that mean?" And it would throw the guy off his autopilot, and he would explain in a sound bite what he was saying. But the most essential things are: 1) do your homework; and 2) listen.

I mean, let's talk about new kids in the business. A few years ago I was at the [*New York*] *Post* [as managing editor]. I got to go to Cuba with Cardinal O'Connor. We land in Cuba, and we're on the bus taking us to Havana, and there's a young woman from the Associated Press. And the entire ride from the airport to the hotel, she's going through her notes. She never looks out the window. She's like the eleventh person in the world to be in Cuba, and she's not looking."

Here we had a reporter—one of a handful of American journalists to travel to Cuba in decades—whose job it was to report for a major wire service what the country was like; yet she never looked out the window to *see* what it was like. It's the visual equivalent of not listening to the answers someone is giving you, but rather focusing on what you're going to ask next. Nachman concludes, "The best questions come from responding to what has been said—and nobody ever listens anymore."

A Matter of Style

As a journalist, I found it was very often stressful to have to ask tough questions of someone I knew I would be dealing with on a regular basis. Everyone wants to be liked, and reporters don't especially want to have rancorous relationships with people they cover regularly. Yet it happens all the time, because it's part of the job. I developed a style whereby I could attribute the tough questions to someone else. For twelve years I did a monthly statewide hour-long broadcast with New York Governor Mario Cuomo. I often had some tough and critical questions to ask him, and he often didn't appreciate them. Still, we maintained a good relationship, because when I asked a tough question, I would frequently couch it in terms like, "Governor, some people are saying . . . blah blah blah." In other words, it wasn't me asking the tough question—I was just passing it on. That way, I never worried about someone saying, "I don't want to go on the air with that SOB. He always asks those tough questions." Rather, I kept getting willing participants, and developed a reputation for being a good and thorough interviewer without rankling egos. But at times it was a nerve-racking job.

I asked Mike Wallace, "How do you get the balls to ask the really tough questions?" "Why shouldn't I?" was his reply. "First of all, I don't have powers of subpoena, and people know who I am and what I do. So they rather expect the difficult or straightforward question."

Does it make the *questioner* nervous, knowing that what's coming is a real bombshell question? Perhaps some questioners, but not Mike Wallace. "I did one this morning. And far from getting nervous, I rather enjoyed taking the person that I'm talking to unawares."

Yet such tough questioning and tough reporting can lead to "kill the messenger syndrome," something *60 Minutes*'s Leslie Stahl runs into often.

And that's part of being a journalist. That's a *big* part of being a journalist, having everybody dislike you for delivering news they don't want to know. I really think that. And I think that part of being a journalist is being able to take it, and saying, "I'm sorry, but I'm not going to shade it because you hate it. I'm going to tell you what I know. I'm not going to know something and censor it because you're not going to like it, and I'm going to keep trying to find out things, because that's my job.

You know, in a democracy, if we don't do it, nobody does it. In a parliamentary system the opposition gets to grill the prime minister and his cabinet. Well, we don't have that system here. We have a system where it's really the press. That's why these officials should be more accountable to us than they are. But I think our job is to be as tough as we can be and to tell the public what we know.

With the responsibility of being tough goes the requirement of being prepared. If you want to go out there and ask those tough questions, you'd better have the information you need, to know what the questions should be and what the answers will mean. Unfortunately, not much of that goes on these days. Most reporters seem ill-prepared, underresearched, and willing to wing it. That is not the way to approach any story. In fact, a question most reporters today don't seem willing to ask is, "I'm sorry, but I don't understand what you mean. Would you explain that to me?" They'd rather fake it than admit they don't know something or didn't do the research. When it comes time to actually do the story, they either get it wrong or totally leave out the part they didn't understand. That's sad for them, and bad for us as news consumers.

Don't Quote Me, But . . .

Media trainers who teach executives how to conduct themselves in interviews always warn their clients that no matter what anybody says, nothing is off the record. In fact, a reporter is always on duty, even as a guest at your house for a Sunday barbeque. Say something casually that's newsworthy, and you're likely to read it in the next day's paper or hear it on the radio the next morning. Like the old story about the scorpion and the frog, that's what reporters do.

I once was reporting on the goings-on at a very secret, very critical political caucus held by a local party committee. In any group, there is always someone who is disgruntled. People like that become sources, and sources are how we get news we can't otherwise get. When we report, we call them "unidentified sources." Sometimes they are also "close to the situation," and very often we add that the very same source—if it happens to be, for example, a party official—"declined to comment" when asked about the information. Generally we won't run a story unless we have two independent sources; such was the case with this particular political report.

So I ran the story of this secret meeting and the political goings-on, and I got a call from a judge who happened to be the subject of the meeting. Actually the politicians were trying to get rid of him, so he had a vested interest in the matter. He was at the meeting, he told me, and while he didn't dispute the accuracy of my report, he was incensed that I would broadcast a story quoting only unnamed sources and insiders. He said journalists had no right to do such a thing. I calmed him down, and just before he hung up he gave me a little political tidbit to use, but he added, "Don't quote me." I checked out the material, used it, and said I got it from "an informed source."

So what about this "off-the-record" stuff? In a book about the Clinton campaign of 1996, author Ken Auletta quotes presidential press secretary Mike McCurry. It seems McCurry had a hard time convincing Clinton to go to the back of the plane and chat with reporters "off the record" for a couple of hours. When he finally prevailed, McCurry went back to tell the campaign press corps about the off-the-record chat opportunity. The *New York Times* reporter remarked, "Fine, off the record unless he makes news."

I asked Mike Wallace if it's important for a reporter to have a personal off-the-record policy.

Sometimes it is. Look, the truth is it's very difficult sometimes to understand what is off the record, what is background, what is deep background. I've had discussions of this nature with all kinds of reporters over the years, particularly Washington reporters. And I've never really fully understood deep background, background, off the record, on the record, when do you go off and how do you get back on, and so forth. And there have been very, very few times—if you understand each other, and you establish a chemistry of confidentiality with your subject—I can count them on less than five fingers, when there's been a misunderstanding. What I will do sometimes, after I've been told this is background or this is on the record or this is off, I will go back over and say, "OK, I want to understand. What have I got here?" I'm not trying to trick anybody or take advantage of anybody.

The credibility of a reporter is his or her stock-in-trade. I have *never* violated a confidence once I've agreed to talk off the record. If I did hear something I felt was exceptionally important to my story, I might try to change the mind of the source or at least get permission to "second source" the story—that is, try to find someone else to tell me the same information *on* the record. When I was working on an investigative piece and needed to convince an interview subject I could be trusted, I always knew I could provide a favorable reference from others who had taken me into their confidence in the past, and I would often do just that.

When Jerry Nachman and I worked the streets of New York City back in the good old days, "off the record" was the name of the classroom we attended every day. I'll let Nachman explain.

We had great teachers; and who were the teachers? [Congressman] Mario Biaggi, [District Attorney and Judge] Burt Roberts, [Brooklyn District Attorney] Gene Gold . . . There was a time when those guys trusted us. Gene Gold would bring us in a room and explain what the indictment was about. No tape recorders, no cameras. And he would walk us through the four corners of the indictment. His bureau chiefs hated it. They were terrified. His squad hated it, 'cause he would say things like, "This time I got the guinea fuck right where I want him." And he'd explain all this. What's a felony? What's a misdemeanor? He'd explain what first-degree manslaughter was versus second-degree manslaughter. See, he understood that the actual news conference was a ceremony, like a bar mitzvah or a wedding. You always have a rehearsal. This briefing was the rehearsal.

He also served bagels, as you remember. But he served bagels for one reason . . . to get the [TV] crews there on time and set up and set-tled down. And then when he was convinced that the reporters understood why we were there, he'd go out and come back in, and there'd be that obligatory shot of him walking down the long confer-ence table, sitting at the head of the table, looking at his papers, say-ing, "I'm announcing today the indictment of one Vinnie Vaselino, 53 years old, of 103 Fifty-third Street in Brooklyn, charged with many counts of felonies, including but not limited to murder, attempted murder, manslaughter, involuntary manslaughter, receiving stolen goods, conspiracy, extortion, and robbery." And it was always my job or [crime reporter] Chris Borgen's job to ask the first question, which never changed: "Mr. Gold, is there any reason to believe that this individual is involved in organized crime?" And Gene Gold would hold up his hand and say, "I cannot go any further than the four corners of this indictment, and it would be inappropriate for me to characterize this defendant or any defendant in such a manner." So it was a ritual. But that session with him doesn't exist anymore. He would never do that now. He's not there, but *nobody* would do that now.

But that was routine. You could go up to someone and they knew they could go off the record with you. Reporters don't want to go off the record today. They think this is somehow prostituting themselves.

Where did this new attitude about off the record come from?

They went to too many movies. They went to journalism school. I don't know.

By the way, please don't repeat any of what you've read here . . . it's off the record.

Sometimes the best question is no question at all. Charles Kuralt, perhaps the pussycat of interviewers, had a way of wringing the last drop of poignancy out of an interview without pressing at all, and he says he took his cue from his polar opposite, Mike Wallace.

We had a small crew. We didn't have producers and researchers and all that, and we didn't take ourselves very seriously. That really helped to put people at their ease. And sometimes, you don't even have to ask a question. You said you talked to Mike Wallace. I've noticed that he asks a question, sometimes gets an answer, and then just sits there smiling at the person. And I think the person feels, "Well, he's not satisfied. I'd better go on." Sometimes, letting someone go on that way elicits the real great line, the revealing remark.

As Wallace himself points out, however, those moments of silence are backed up by hours of research and planning, which also give him what he needs to ask those irreverent questions.

First of all, you've done research. I write a lot of my questions, not just to be ready to have the next question, but also because in writing questions I am learning about the story. I mean, I'll go through the research and I'll think, "This would be interesting," and I'll write it down. And sometimes I'll do a category: money, ambition, mistakes, and so forth. And I'll write down maybe fifty questions before an interview, questions based on stuff that I had read or seen on television about that individual.

Being loaded for bear, Wallace proceeds with the interview in such a way as to relax the interview subject and make him or her feel comfortable—as well as confident that Wallace has done his homework and knows his stuff. The skill is in knowing when the chemistry is just at the right point to ask those tough questions. "After a while," he remarks, "it becomes second nature. In fact, that's all technique."

The backbone of any good interview is knowledge. Brian Williams says the key is *reading*.

My vocation and avocation are the same thing. So it's not an effort for me to remain current on as many possible subjects as I can. The night TWA 800 went down, I had to talk [anchoring the news desk on NBC] for six hours. No one was going to help me. Because I was the kind of kid who kept the fold-out issue of the 1969 *Popular Science* about the new jumbo jet that was coming soon from Boeing, I was able to rely on a body of knowledge, being an aviation buff all my life. I was fortunate. Had it been an equestrian accident, I wouldn't have known as much. But it was an aircraft accident, so I had enough to talk about for six hours. I knew the questions to ask. That's the other part: You have to know enough so you know what to ask, and you have to know what you *don't* know.

In addition to knowing what to ask, Williams notes, it's also important to know what questions *not* to ask.

That varies from person to person and from issue to issue. There are questions that are still beyond the bounds of propriety in the twenty-first century. I think certain personal behavior that's not germane to a person's performance, not germane to a person's job, is beyond those bounds. Family privacy issues. A fascinating question to examine is: Just five decades after the news media refused to show Roosevelt being lifted from his car, we voluntarily backed away from Chelsea Clinton. Sitting here talking to you, I know a hell of a lot about Chelsea Clinton. I know all about her. I've never said it on the air. I know whom she's dating. I know where he lives. I know all about her personal life. Who her Secret Service detail is. What she does after school. Where she learned to drive, and with whom. But at the request of the First Family and believing that it is not germane to coverage of the president, I've chosen to leave her alone. I'm also a parent. I have a daughter. I would appreciate that same treatment.

Egad! Do I detect a note of sensitivity in a big-time journalist? Can this be? Well, yes it can. In fact, to be really good at this job, sensitivity is probably a necessary trait. I mean, Walter Cronkite is a sensitive guy.

Well, I think it certainly helps. I think it's particularly important to understand where people are coming from, in the current phrase. Who they are. What their backgrounds are. How they got to where they are. Why they perform the way they do. This should be part of our inquisitiveness, part of our desire to round the story out completely. It doesn't necessarily mean you're going to report all those facts or try to put them into your story. But it will give you a better lead on the "why" of the story, which is the mystery element. Who, what, when, and where are obvious. "Why" gets to be the difficult question.

And "why" is probably the most important question a reporter can ask.

Why?

Funny you should ask.

I I

GET YOUR NEWS FROM US
~WE'RE NOT TOO BAD!~

A ndy Rooney and I share an interest in woodworking. I have made a table, some kitchen cabinets, and a few doors, and I've even built a building or two in my day, including my well-equipped and spacious workshop. Now I don't know about Andy, but I come from the woodworking school founded by that famous Russian, Boris Goodenuf. I'm always rushing to get finished, and many times I will look at my project and say, "Good enough." However, that is my *hobby*, not my profession. I don't try to sell my work to anyone, and I have to please only myself—OK, and my wife, whose criticism I can usually assuage by telling her, "It's good enough, and maybe I'll fix it later." But when you're broadcasting news to millions of people, "good enough" isn't good enough, and fixing it later is going to be too late.

I actually had this conversation with a boss of mine, after convincing him to take me to lunch at a fine Chinese restaurant near the CBS headquarters building in midtown Manhattan. It was a favorite spot for both of us, because the food was excellent, as was the service—that's why we kept going back there. More often than not, when rushing to a story I would eat a hot dog from one of those dreaded street corner vendors. It wasn't gourmet, but it was good enough.

Now here's an approximation of how that luncheon conversation went between the boss and me. In this scene, I play myself. Note: Portions of this conversation have been edited or condensed in the interest of your time and my space, and because I can't remember exactly how it went.

ATHENS: I'm really concerned about the quality of our product. I think it's going downhill.

BOSS: Give me an example.

ATHENS: That series we ran last week was poorly produced and totally lacked substance. The pieces were so short, it was impossible to get any useful points across or even make it remotely interesting to listen to. On top of that, you barely gave the reporter enough time to research, write, and produce it. It wasn't fair to the listeners, because they could get nothing out of it. It was a waste of their time, and that's not fair.

BOSS: Oh, *that* series. I heard it. It wasn't so bad. Give me another example.

ATHENS: (I gave him another example.)

BOSS: Oh, yes. I heard that. It was OK.

ATHENS: (In smart-ass tone:) Oh, is that our new slogan now? "Listen to us, we're not so bad." Or, "When you need news, tune us in—we're OK"? What happened to things like excellence, or the best we can be? What's our goal now? What will the coach tell us in the locker room: "OK guys, let's go out there and show them we can be not too bad"? Our slogan used to be "The Best in the Business!" (It really was.)

The conversation went on like that. The boss said he understood my concerns but didn't necessarily agree with them, but he said he would "look into it." He also picked up the check. A few months later, he called me into his office and asked me if I could do a revisit to a topic I had won a Peabody Award for some years before. I had done a ten-part series on the taxi industry in New York, and the scandalous way in which the Taxi and Limousine Commission handled cab drivers who continued to drive and thrive while ripping off hundreds of tourists for thousands of dollars. I had spent, on and off, six months researching that series, and each part of the broadcast ran three and a half minutes. My boss (Mr. Notsobad) now wanted me to spend about two weeks on it and do one- to one-and-a-half-minute pieces. "Quick and dirty" is the way he described it. "Quick and dirty" to me means, "Don't waste much time on this—after all, it's only for our listeners, and they won't notice if it's not excellent. Everyone else sucks, so it's OK if we do, too. Why knock yourself out? Just make it good enough to fool people into thinking we've given them something worthwhile. They won't know the difference." I wonder how the food in that Chinese restaurant would taste if the owners and chefs and waiters decided to take care of their customers in a "quick and dirty" way. How many of their customers would come back?

Substance Makes the Smart Go Wander

Ed Ingles—long-time, big-time sportscaster in New York and on CBS Sports—used to joke about squeezing the proverbial ten pounds of sports into a five-pound sportscast. "Leave out the verbs," he'd quip. Ingles knew that on a Monday, after all those football games and maybe a tennis tournament and some baseball trades, it was not possible to do more than give the scores in the two and a half minutes he had for his broadcast. Eventually that was cut to two minutes, even as the leagues were expanding. So many scores; so little time. There's the classic "And now the scores: four to three, eight to five, and sixteen to nothing. In other sports news today . . ." But that's a joke . . . or is it?

The news has shrunk. Where has all the substance gone? It has gone into commercials, and it has gone into increasing story count. On *60 Minutes*, where they once had fifteen or sixteen minutes for a story, they now have only thirteen. On news radio stations WCBS and WINS in New York City, the commercials are, for the most part, 25 to 50 percent longer than the stories they surround. It takes longer to hawk a headache cure than it does to explain the nuances of the presidential election. News stories have become teases.

It used to be that a news story told you who, what, when, where, how, and why. Now the story might tell you who, or it might tell you when, but there's a good chance that when it's over (which won't take long), *you'll* be the one saying, "What?" A number of years ago, management people thought they had to have more stories on the air than the competition. Of course, the only people actually counting the stories were management people. At WCBS, the stories tended to run longer and have more depth than they did at WINS. But as WCBS increased its story count to "keep up" with the WINS story count, the stories got shorter and shorter. The "in-depth" reports got shallower and shallower. Now they are pretty much gone, and so is an army of listeners. As of this writing, the ratings for WCBS are less than half what they were back in the days when it was known as "the best in the business." Where have all the listeners gone? They've gone where the substance went. Away.

Of course there are listeners who don't want substance, don't care, don't want to know more about it. But many are tired of mumbling, "Huh?" under their breath at the end of every story they see or hear. So they've wandered off to places like public radio—whose stories can be somewhat irrelevant to everyday life in Brooklyn, but are generally quite thorough and well-produced. And to public television broadcasts like *The NewsHour with Jim Lehrer*. Many have turned to the Internet, where they can get all the detail they want. Some people have gone back to newspapers like the *New York Times*. Broadcast television viewing, including of the news, is way down, and you have to wonder if people have decided it's just not worth their time.

A Penny for a Complete Thought?

I hear or see something every once in a while that makes me just want to laugh out loud, or cry quietly to myself. I often jot down these events in case I ever decide to write another book. Now we all know that a man-bites-dog story is newsworthy. Would that make a man-*shoots*-dog story more or *less* newsworthy? Whichever, this one made my list.

It seems a pit bull in the Bronx was menacing some police who were in the process of making an arrest. The dog apparently attacked one of the cops, who then shot the animal dead. It made the news.

Two days later in a New York City suburb, another cop . . . another pit bull . . . another shot fired ... another dead dog. Wow. Two in one week. This *really* made the news. In fact, on one TV station it was the lead story, and it went something like this:

"A police officer was blah, blah, blah, when a pit bull attacked him and blah, blah, blah, and the dog is dead." Now, here's the important part: The anchor said with great emphasis, "This happened just two days after a dog died in the Bronx." End of story.

Is there something missing here, or is it just me? There simply was no time to explain that another policeman shot another dog in a similar circumstance in the Bronx just two days before? That would have given perspective and substance to the story, but there just wasn't time for it. If someone had been out of town and had just come back, their perspective would have been that a dog died in the Bronx, and they would be wondering to this day (perhaps some still are) about what a dog dying in the Bronx had to do with a suburban policeman. Dogs die in the Bronx all the time. To me it's just like, "Today's scores are four to three, eight to five, and sixteen to nothing."

There are millions of stories like that. Stories without substance. You watch a story for two minutes and you say to yourself, "Why did I waste my time? I still don't know anything." I hate that. So does ABC's Lynn Sherr.

Right. And worse than that is the story that *has* some substance, where the subject is really substantive, but they never lay it out for you. That drives me crazy. If I'm anything as a reporter, I'm very clear. You watch a piece I've done, and you will totally understand what I've told you. I'm not being unhumble. It's what I do. I can look at a complicated thing and make it understandable. And it makes me crazy when other people don't do that. When I watch a piece, I sit there and I edit. Why wasn't that up at the top? Where's that information? It's because they're getting bad editing, and because some of the people at the top are not demanding that clarity.

Why is that?

I think there are not a lot of mentors. I think there are people in the business who do not have a good, solid background, and they're going for the written glitz and razzle-dazzle and the *appearance* of journalism. You know, kind of journalism lite, pseudojournalism . . . fake journalism. I don't know what it is. And it passes as good reporting. It's not. You know, I don't think it's even adequate.

It may not be adequate, but it is . . . good enough. And for many, both behind the scenes and in front of the camera, good enough is all they strive for. Sherr has a case in point:

Years ago when I was at [ABC's] *World News* [*Tonight*], I did a piece on—it was an obit, I believe it was Eugene Ormandy. Now, number one, we would never do Ormandy today . . . you wouldn't do an obit on Ormandy. At least we did it. And you know the mode, you get in in the morning, you find out the guy has just died, you collect all the video, you get the film, the this, the that, you get the clips; and I knew something about the man. The producer was a young man (which is relevant), and we finished the piece. I think it was the days when we had a six o'clock, a 6:30, and a seven o'clock feed. So we made the six o'clock feed and it was fairly high in the show, for whatever reason. We were on the air and just made it; and we're sitting there and we're watching the piece. He's watching, and I said, "You know, I think I did the wrong lead." And he looked at me and said, "What do you mean?" "I think I did the wrong lead." He said, "What are you talking about? We made air." And there it was in a nutshell. I was a little concerned, perhaps overly so, that I had written the wrong first sentence, that I should have cast the story a slightly different way. I honestly don't remember why. But I distinctly remember that he was baffled: He did not have a clue about what I was talking about. All he cared about was making air. I, of course, cared about making air, but I also cared about the substance, about making my point, and about what was I telling 20 million people, or whatever the number was that were watching that night.

But, Lynn . . . it was good enough. Just like the story I saw the other night about a man who was arrested for squeezing bread in a supermarket. It seems the guy always came around and squeezed the bread—I don't know why—and finally he was arrested for it. They never explained why he did it or exactly why he was arrested, but in the middle of the piece, they had a sound bite of a woman, unidentified, who said something like, "It's terrible. I get home and I'm tired and then I have to go back to the store because of him." Words to that effect. What did it all mean? They never explained, but that woman probably had something to do with the store where the bread was being squeezed. I suppose I could have called the station to ask, but I probably would have gotten someone who would explain that however they did the story, it was surely good enough.

Which brings me to another thing. Have you noticed how many times, especially on the local news, they show pictures over a story that seem to have nothing to do with what they're talking about? Could be a fire story, and they'll show cars parked on the street or a woman standing in a doorway or a dog sniffing a tree. Just a bunch of pictures, while the anchor goes on about the flames and the smoke and the collapsing roof. To get to the bottom of this we talked with Bill Bauman, a long-time news director and currently general manager at the NBC affiliate WESH in Orlando, Florida.

> You know why? It's laziness. It's fundamentally laziness. You've got a producer who writes the voice-over[1] or the headline in the computer and shoots it off to a tape editor with the instruction, "I need twenty seconds of the fire." Only nobody's reading the script and saying, "Can we pick twenty seconds that kind of match what I'm talking about?" So you end up with a woman standing in the doorway or cars parked or a dog instead of the great flames shooting through the roof, because an editor says, "Yeah, twenty seconds, just rip off twenty seconds." It's a structural laziness. You won't see that from a good producer, because a good producer will send it off in the computer, then get up and walk into the tape room and say, "Let's print this thing I just wrote and let's look at the video, and let's make sure it all matches up." A lot of kids don't do that anymore—and I don't know if they're lazy or harried. I think it's both."

And *I* think it's because they figure it's good enough—and no one discourages them from thinking that way.

SIZE *IS* IMPORTANT!

Getting back to this quick and dirty business. The once in-depth, three-minute pieces I used to do on WCBS Radio are no more. It seems that, to management, forty-five seconds is a long piece. Increased commercial load and an insistent rant about traffic and weather, even on clear Sundays and holiday weekends, take a toll of time away from news.

1 Voice-over: The script read by the anchor while pictures are shown on the screen.

Self-promotion takes another bite. "Listen to us, we're not so bad . . . ta-rah ta-rah." There is little time to actually do the news any justice. I remember when the Clinton impeachment hearings were going on. WCBS, the flagship all-news station of the so-called "Tiffany" network, decided it would run the Clinton deposition live. They ran Clinton, all right—in two- and three-minute bits and pieces, interrupting for commercials, traffic, sports, and business news. It was senseless. You couldn't even figure out the gist of Clinton's testimony. But it was good enough. That decision, by the way, was made by the same manager who ordered anchors to run the "breaking story" sounder every time they reported *old* news on an *old* story that hadn't had a new angle to it for a day and a half. When an anchor questioned him about it, saying it was misleading, the manager said something to the effect of "Yeah, but it sounds *great*." By the way, that manager is gone. The anchor still rules.

ATHENS'S FIRST LAW: The amount of useful information you can get out of a story is directly proportional to the amount of time the story is given on the air.

ATHENS'S SECOND LAW: All stories are not equal. Some aren't worth much time; others are.

I'm sorry to say that there are very few people enforcing these laws. In fact, an obsession with "story count"—that is, airing as many stories as possible in the shortest amount of time—has led to making almost all stories equal in length. You see it all the time with what has become a popular bit on local television news. It's referred to as "Eleven at eleven," and what it means is that they'll actually give you eleven minutes of news without stopping. That news may include a promotional tie-in to the entertainment show you watched earlier on that same network, and it might include a weather tease: "It's going to be *cold* tonight. How cold? Cold enough to kill your tomato plants? Maybe. We'll tell you later."

The general rule for reporters these days is something like: "You've got forty-five seconds. You've got a minute and a half." What's the story about? Doesn't matter. There are plenty of other stories to get on, so they each get the same deal. After all, there are considerations other than the importance of the story or what's needed to tell it right: There are reporters' egos. "How come she always gets more time than I do?"

It wasn't egos but quality that played a role in determining how long a Charles Kuralt "On the Road" piece would run on the *CBS Evening News with Walter Cronkite.* "Brevity is the biggest single problem today," Kuralt notes.

"On the Road" stories routinely used to run four or five minutes— once as long as seven and a half, when we did San Francisco cable cars. Of course, seven and a half minutes, when you allow for commercials, is about one-third of the evening news." (Actually, today it would be more than a third.)

How did they get a story that long on the air? It certainly wasn't by worrying about story count.

I happened to be back in New York, hanging over the editor's shoulder, working on that one, and it was just so pretty and somehow it came out well rounded: It had a beginning, a middle, and an end, and the producer hated to mess it up. So he just waited for a night when there wasn't much else to talk about and put it on. But brevity, to the extent to which it's practiced in broadcasting today, makes it impossible to tell most stories with the kind of feeling that engages the listener. The evening news shows I see and even the interviews they do in the morning—they don't run long enough. The thing you hear most often on those shows is, "Well, we're out of time . . . we have to leave it there . . . thanks for joining us."

"I'm right now undertaking a new TV project for this coming year to try to do ninety-second stories, syndicated to stations. They're about Americana: one discrete, one single subject: cowboy hats; barber poles; manhole covers; old stone walls. You can just about do that—a fair job—in about a minute and a half. But they tried, for example, a cowboy singer who's preserving genuine old songs of the West. That you cannot do. You cannot do that in a minute and a half. You can't do it and let him sing half a song, much less hear him talking. So that one we just killed. It would have been a lovely six- or seven-minute story, but you have to stick to Niagara Falls in winter— "Look, isn't it pretty"; you can just about do that in a minute and a half.

Kuralt says there are obvious reasons why a good story needs time to unfold.

First of all, you have to care about the story yourself. You have to be persuaded that what you're doing is not wasting the listener's or viewer's time. You have to be genuinely interested. And if you're not, if you don't have the kind of curiosity that makes you genuinely interested in nearly everything that you're apt to approach, then you ought to be in the wholesale grocery business or something—you know, a different line of work. It's not a crime; it's just a different mindset. And then you have to have time to give your viewer the insight that makes you so interested in the story. That takes a little while. I mean, it doesn't take forever, and you can make it a fairly brief process, but you have to give people an understanding of where they are and who this is and why this is so interesting. And you just can't do it in a few seconds.

SPEAKING OF MANAGERS, AND WE WERE . . .

Sometimes the boss is wrong. In order to determine when that is, an employee has to be able to know the difference between right and wrong. Then that employee has to be willing to *fight* for what is right and oppose what is wrong—has to be willing to stake his or her job on it. Failure to do so can lead to mediocrity, and we all know where that can lead. The people who have really achieved their own personal level of excellence are willing to take responsibility for the quality of the work they are in any way connected with. Dan Rather, for example, has a rule about that.

Here's what's worked for me. I believe in the ten magic words, which are: "If it is to be, it is up to me." My work is up to me. If my work is to be excellent, if it is to be, it is up to me. You might find yourself in a situation in which you say, "I have to face it; mediocrity is good enough for the boss. Either he or she doesn't know the difference, and/or they're not willing to pay for the difference." I don't like to work in an environment with mediocrity, and I'll say more about that in a moment. I think one should, within reason, really strive to stay out of situations in which you're in an environment of mediocrity.

Because it's that old story my mother used to tell me: "If you hang around a pool hall long enough, you're going to start picking up the habits of the people there." Well, so it is when you work in an atmosphere of mediocrity. But here's the important part to say to yourself: "I can achieve individual excellence here, even in this environment of mediocrity." It's tougher. It's a greater challenge, it's more demanding, and you'll be disappointed much more often. It takes determination in yourself—"I'm not going to be mediocre." You need to have a slogan. I'm not suggesting you wear a tee shirt, but to, in your imagination, have a tattoo on your chest that says, "Adequate is inadequate." To sort of practice your craft with that as your code will help you.

Well, you might be thinking, it's easy for someone like Dan Rather to say that. But remember, Dan Rather wasn't always the Dan Rather you think of today.

I do know the reality—it's very important to me that you know, and whoever is reading this knows—I understand the pressures. I have been there, done that, and bought the tee shirt. I know what it is to work in an environment in which everybody says, "Listen, Dan, you may have these fantasies of quality, you may have this polar star out there, this excellence, but let me tell you, I want five pieces today, and the main thing for me is that you come back with five pieces." I do understand that, and that makes it difficult to say to yourself, "Adequate is inadequate. I want to be excellent, and it's up to me." But if the environment becomes such that you feel that you cannot even strive for personal excellence, then you have to move. Even if it's costly—I fully understand that. Again . . . been there . I've got a wife, kids, car payments, and a mortgage. It's very difficult to struggle with these things. It's very easy if you're Dan Rather to talk about them in the abstract, but it's important to me for you to know that it hasn't always been such.

Quitting is a big decision. It does something to your inner self to quit. So a lot of times if you just struggle on, just fight on, just keep putting one foot in front of the other, even in a bad situation, you will find that you can break through and are able to do something—if not excellent, then something pretty close to it.

Rather isn't suggesting that a journalist must spend an entire career swimming upstream against a tide of management indifference to quality. However, it is true that the stronger swimmers are the ones who will make it to the spawning grounds. Once there, it means they have earned the right to be creative and at least somewhat true to themselves. But even the big-timers like Mike Wallace clash with their bosses over form or content. The twenty-fifth anniversary broadcast of 60 Minutes opened with an argument between Wallace and 60 Minutes honcho Don Hewitt. They are in a heated debate over a story Wallace had prepared for that week's broadcast. The nugget of that argument was Wallace protesting, "Oh come on, Don. For chrissake, you're gutting the piece."

Wallace argues over Hewitt's staccato—"Mike, Mike, Mike, Mike, Mike." He continues to push his point. Hewitt throws down his pencil, angrily stands up, and says, "Then forget 60 Minutes. You don't get on this week!"

Yes, the great Mike Wallace and the all-powerful Don Hewitt were arguing like a cub reporter and an unsympathetic editor at a college paper. But the argument was steeped in passion, the kind of passion that makes for excellence. Hewitt admits that usually Wallace was right. But Wallace didn't always win. I recall arguing passionately with my boss over some story or other, an argument I seemed unable to steer my way. I finally said, "OK, you win. I'll do it your way—not because you are right, but because you are the boss." I felt defeated, save for the smart-ass last word I managed to salvage, but it didn't deter me from putting up a fight the next time. Sometimes, I won, and it was all worth it.

Is Your Underwear Showing?

I spent much of my career doing investigative journalism, which often leads a reporter down potentially libelous paths. That's why TV networks and stations have lawyers. Lawyers would vet stories for potential liability—and if things looked too dicey, very often the lawyers would say, "Forget it. That's not going on our air." One of the more notorious such cases involved CBS lawyers and the 60 Minutes tobacco industry exposé based on information provided by an ex–tobacco company executive. The ex-employee had signed a nondisclosure agreement when he left Phillip Morris, and CBS lawyers feared that they would be accused by the tobacco company of enticing or encouraging the informant to violate that agreement. They would sue, said Phillip Morris's lawyers—exposing CBS to perhaps billions in liability at a time when the network was in negotiations for its sale. So the story was killed—all of which led to the movie *The Insider*, but that's another story altogether. The point I'm trying to make is that lawyers tend to kill stories, and reporters are ill equipped to argue the legal issues with them.

I had a boss once who believed that although lawyers thought they were around to keep broadcasters out of trouble, their actual function should be to *get* broadcasters out of trouble after the fact. Otherwise, he reasoned, journalism would lose its edge by playing it too safe. Yet, there are bosses who just want *to* play it safe. Charles Osgood remembers a boss like that.

> At WCBS radio, I started doing commentary pieces at 8:20 in the morning that were repeated on the air at 11:20 in the morning. And they started to attract a little attention. People were looking forward to them, and among the people whose attention they attracted was Bill Paley [CBS founder and chairman]. On several occasions, he would call down, or someone from his office would call down, and say, "Mr. Paley would like to have a copy of the 8:20 piece." The routine was that it would be played back later in the morning, at 11:20. And on each occasion when he called, it was because he *liked* it. He liked it a lot, and he wanted to see it and share it with somebody. Whatever the reason, he wanted it because he liked it. But even though that happened again and again, every time Mr. Paley requested a copy of the piece, the boss would cancel the second feed of it [the 11:20 broadcast], just in case he *didn't* like it. Because the first priority for the boss was, Don't do anything somebody doesn't like. "He probably likes it, but what if he doesn't?" If Paley *did* like it, then the boss could say, "Thank you very much. I'm glad you liked it." But if he *didn't* like it, then he could say, "I couldn't agree with you more, Mr. Paley. In fact, we canceled the second feed of that broadcast because we certainly didn't want to air *that* again."

Some "cover your ass" routine, wasn't it? Senseless but safe. And what could Osgood do about it?

Well, I wasn't in a position to do anything about it, but I felt that the reason he did that was because, if you're running scared, then you don't want to stick out. Because if you stick out, what if they don't like it? If you stick out, they're going to say, "What are you doing with poems on the radio? Get out of here!" You're taking a chance. Whenever you do anything that's different, you run the risk of somebody not liking it. And probably, somebody *isn't* going to like it."

That risk, as Osgood has proven over the years, is worth it. Go for the gold. Be more than just OK.

TAKE TWO ANECDOTES AND CALL ME IN THE MORNING

It was a dark and boring night. I was passing the time watching the 11:00 p.m. local news out of Albany, New York. It seems that some time during the day a huge *moose* had wandered from the forest primeval and into a suburban Albany neighborhood. People looked out of their windows and said, "What's a moose like you doing in a place like this?" Soon the police were called, and the animal control people were called, and the environmental people were called, and of course the TV stations were called. In the suburbs of Albany, a moose on the loose is a big story. So they chased the moose around for a few hours and finally . . . well, let me tell it the way the reporter told it—live—standing in the dark in a suburban neighborhood hours after the event was over.

She explained—as videotape from earlier in the day played on the screen—that they finally shot the moose with a heavy-duty tranquilizer. After it collapsed, they were able to use a harness to lift the moose onto a truck and transport it back to the forest whence it came.

OK, now cut back to the "live" picture of the reporter standing in the dark. She says, smiling, "Reporting live from the scene, I'm (name withheld by me out of charity). Now back to you in the studio."

Cut to split screen. Anchor on left, reporter in the dark on right. The anchor says something like, "Thanks for that report. But could they just let the moose go after giving it a tranquilizer and knocking it out?" Cut to full screen of reporter in the dark, who, with great conviction, asserts, "Oh no. Before they released it, they gave it an anecdote. Back to you."

The anchor said: "Thanks."

I said to my wife, "These two moose went into a bar . . . ," but, alas, my voice trailed off, for I didn't know any moose anecdotes—at least, not until this story happened.

Sound far-fetched? It happens all the time. Could it have been a slip of the tongue that caused the reporter to say *anecdote* instead of *antidote?* The anchor seemed satisfied with the chosen word. It was good enough. Now, in fairness, that was *live* television. Such a thing could never happen in an *edited* piece, could it?

Dean Daniels is a former CBS News executive who has moved on to the technological wonders of the dot.com world. He recalls his early days at WTRF in Wheeling, West Virginia. As Dean tells it:

> We had this one reporter, and I won't name any names, who went out to cover the Barnsville Pumpkin Festival, which is a big deal out there. Back then the interviews weren't fifteen-second sound bites; you had to fill an hour of news, so the interview should go forty-five seconds. So the reporter was interviewing this farmer who's the organizer of the festival, moving the mike back and forth between them and asking him a few questions. About the third question, the reporter says, "And about how often do you hold this annual event?" The farmer looks at the reporter, looks sideways, a chaw in his mouth, and says, "Oh, about once a year." And it aired! And I mean, I'm sitting there watching this in the newsroom, and this intern is saying, "How can this happen? How can this be happening?"

Doug Poling, a former CBS News colleague, e-mailed word from the great city of Nashville: Harry Belafonte was in town for a series of appearances. Poling wrote: "One of Belafonte's appearances was at a news conference to promote prostate cancer screening. (He's a survivor of the disease.) Belafonte told the assembled reporters, "All men over the age of 40 should be screened for prostate cancer." At which point a female reporter from Channel 2 (ABC) commented, "Yes, and women should be checked, too."

Another antidote, I mean anecdote, this from the City of Brotherly Love. Shortly after the release of the film *Malcolm X*, his widow, Betty Shabazz, died. An anchor doing a story on her death announced sadly, "The widow of Malcolm Ten has died." Wait—don't laugh. It's not funny; it's sad. Remember, most people get their news from their local station, so what airs there is important.

Just a minute—Dean Daniels is tugging at my sleeve with yet another story.

> DANIELS: Same reporter as the once-a-year story, anchoring. The Vietnam War is ending. The lead-in reads, "Good evening. The GIs are coming home." Roll theme, roll film of GIs, cue the anchor, who says, "Good evening, the G-ones are coming home." Here's a person who obviously had been reading scripts throughout the length of the Vietnam War and I guess had never heard them referred to as GIs."
>
> ATHENS: Now what does that tell you?
>
> DANIELS: It tells me that no matter what the circumstance, there's always room for mediocrity. There will always be mediocrity no matter how much you strive to avoid it. Just right now, I think we have more than our share.

I ended the interview here. It was good enough.

« One good word is worth a thousand pictures. »

ERIC SEVEREID, CBS NEWS COMMENTATOR

12

IT'S THE WRITING, STUPID!
~THE PEN IS MIGHTIER THAN THE PICTURE~

When *60 Minutes* executive producer Don Hewitt watches a
piece he is screening for broadcast, he closes his eyes.

Well, I'll tell you something—I think the one thing we know that
nobody else knows: It is your ear more than your eye that keeps you at
the television set. It's what you *hear*. The picture may get you there; it's
what you *hear* that keeps you there. If you're watching a space launch,
they're poor pictures—they're all the same pictures. And there's
Jennings, there's Brokaw, and there's Rather; and you like Rather, so
you're watching Rather. If they lose the picture—if they put up one of
those signs that says, "We've lost our picture. We'll be back, etc.," you
don't go away, 'cause you're listening to Rather. But if they lose the
audio, you're gone. You don't stay and watch television when there is
no audio. See, I can live with an out-of-focus picture. I can live with a
grainy picture. I can live with a badly framed picture. But I can't live
with grainy audio, out-of-focus audio, or badly framed audio.

Of course, the audio includes the interview and the ambient sound—
but, most important, the writing. "Tell me a story" is Don Hewitt's con-

stant entreaty to his troops. And the telling of that story hangs not on the picture, but on the writing.

> I tell anybody who wants to come into television, "You want to learn this craft? Go work in radio." Work in radio because TV is a *sound* medium more than a picture medium. Anybody can learn pictures. You get a good cameraman, you get a good tape editor—your cameraman is gonna frame the stuff right, he's gonna shoot it well. Learn how to *write*. Every time I speak to a journalism class, I always say to these kids, "There are two ways to write. One is to write for the written word, and the other is to write for the spoken word. You want to know how to write for the spoken word? You go get the [Ed] Murrow and [Fred] Friendly *I Can Hear It Now* recordings, and you listen to the writing. You listen to lines like, "If you've ever been in the jungle at night, you'd know that when a Howitzer screams, the jungle screams back." Learn to write like that and you'll make it.

Indeed, radio is the canvas upon which the imagination can paint pictures so vivid they bring tears to the eyes. The homeless Vietnam vet whose raggedly gloved hand reaches out to touch the newly dedicated memorial wall, tears streaming down his weatherworn face. The surge of emotion rippling through the crowd at West Point as Americans held hostage in Iran first arrived back in the United States: busloads of hostages rumbling slowly past a crowd of thousands who had waited hours to welcome their countrymen home. People standing on tiptoe for a glimpse of the passing buses, waving tiny flags, shedding tears of joy and pride. Such moments are meant to be told.

I often told young reporters that the devil is in the details, and that to truly give life to a story those details must be included. One of the best at bringing a listener to the scene is New York radio reporter Rich Lamb, who would describe the flag snapping in the breeze and the bite of autumn air on tear-stained faces as they watched the funeral procession of a fallen cop.

Some years ago, a cub reporter who worked for me wanted to anchor coverage of a live parade broadcast. It took him a while, but he finally won me over. It was his first parade. Describing a parade on the radio is difficult at best, but he couldn't wait to do it. I reminded him that his job was to bring listeners to the parade in their mind's eye. Details, I explained again, would make the difference—the more the merrier. I urged him to let his mind go and to be creative, no matter how trivial a detail might seem at the moment. Costumes, floats, spectators, little kids perched on their dads' shoulders for a better view—it all helped make the picture complete. So the reporter went on the air live from the parade and intoned, with all the sincerity he could muster: ". . . and here comes the queen of the parade riding on a white stallion." (Pause.) "I think it's a stallion." (Longer pause.) Yes . . . it's a stallion."

So it went, on the radio. On television, you have to work with pictures. A radio reporter colleague of mine, an excellent writer who could captivate listeners with his storytelling, decided to make the transition to television reporting. It didn't work. For one thing, his words were so descriptive they overwhelmed the pictures. Describing a raging fire in detail while at the same time showing exactly what is being described has a way of making the words seem superfluous.

There has to be a fine balance between words and pictures, a balance mastered by the legendary Charles Kuralt.

Something that I feel strongly about is that once you've shot your story and you sit down to write it, you should be writing every sentence to a picture you know is there. I used to be sure that the person who was going to edit the film knew what picture I had in mind when I wrote each line, because you can't do it the other way. You can't write a line and hope that there will be a picture to go with it. That's fundamental, I think. I learned that from Alice Wheel, who was a writer on the *Douglas Edwards Show* back in the fifties. She said, "The picture is so strong that nobody will listen to you unless your words complement the picture."

When you watched a Kuralt piece on the air, he made it seem so easy. It wasn't. There was a lot of hard-earned wisdom behind every stroke on the keyboard.

I think writing is derivative. I think it comes from good writers you've read. I think when you sit down to write, you hear in your mind the rhythms of those good writers—you know, E. B. White, Mark

Twain, Red Smith, and all the writers you've ever admired and been delighted by. And then, I think, your writing is a little bit imitative—not of any one writer, but just of a way of putting it. And it's hard—at least it is for me; I have to sweat it out. I mean, I don't *have* to; I can do a story quickly at conventions and things like that. I frequently did. But I like to be able to take a lot of time. Another good lesson was in Mark Twain's remark, "The difference between the right word and the second-best word is the difference between lightning and a lightning bug." And he, of course, gave us lightning with his choice of words.

It seems sometimes that the people writing broadcast news today don't even have the sense to come in out of the rain, much less give us lightning. If we're lucky, we may get a sun shower. I am amazed at how many young journalists out there today don't like to write and aren't interested in writing. When they write, and often when they anchor or report a news story, it is clear they do not understand what they are writing or talking about. And understanding the material is rule number one. Ask Charles Osgood, one of broadcasting's best writers.

Take fledgling writers. You'll say, "Rewrite this [news] wire copy." So they take the wire copy and they look at the first sentence, and they rewrite the first sentence. Then they look at the second sentence, and they rewrite the second sentence. And when they're finished, they say, "I rewrote the story." That's not the way to do it. The way you do it is, you look at that story and read it. Read it from top to bottom. Then, put it down and start telling that story, and when you come to the part where you need to know the name of the guy . . . then you look back to get the name. But if you don't have the story, I mean the whole story, in your head, you can't possibly tell it. You have to know and understand the story. Then you know where to start and you know where to finish and what you're driving at.

Osgood points out that in broadcasting, unlike in newspapers, the *end* of the story is every bit as important as the beginning.

Print is suspended in space, so that if there's a "Continued on page 17" then you're going to lose a lot of people, because they're not going to make the turn with you. And there's a difference between the top of the page and the bottom of the page. But in broadcasting, everything is suspended in time; it all gets the same exposure. So the last thing you say is just is as important as the first thing you say. It's probably even more important, because that's what you're looking for—the end of the story. I used to suggest writing the first line, then writing the last line. And on the computer, it's very easy to do that. Then you just write, to get to that last line, all of the stuff that you have to say to get where you're going.

Some of broadcasting's finest writers never thought about TV, videotape, or sound bites. All Andy Rooney thought about early on was *writing.*

> I always wanted to be a good writer. I was thinking about how we all study and plan our lives, and what we end up being is not what we studied and planned for. We still have to plan, but something happens that changes everything. I wanted to be a writer before I ever heard of television, and here I end up doing most of my writing for television and I had to adapt my style. I mean, no one speaks as he writes and no one writes as he speaks. So if you're writing for television, you've got to find some way to compromise between your speaking style and your writing style. It can't be one or the other. Speaking style is too discursive. It's repetitive. And writing style is too stiff to speak aloud. So you find some middle ground.

When I write, I hear what I'm writing before I put it down on paper. I guess you could say I write for the ear. When I read a book by Charles Kuralt, I can almost hear him *saying* the words to me. I can hear his voice. Andy Rooney also hears himself saying what he's writing. But when we ad-lib on the air we just say what we hear, rather than putting it down on paper first. It's a strange process, but it just seems to happen with broadcast people.

Then there's the issue of second-guessing yourself: fine-tuning and fine-tuning the same sentence over and over like some great classic novelist. Rooney says that if he has a good idea he writes from the gut, but that doesn't always work.

I do two columns a week in 125 newspapers. I can write a good column in an hour, an hour and a half, eight hundred words. If I do a column that isn't very good, it very often takes me all day. I fuss with it,
I rewrite it, I throw stuff out, I print it off the computer; I look at it,
take it apart, and put it back together again. Usually my better
columns are the ones that I have done most quickly. I don't know why
that is. I'm fussing with one now. It's never going to be very good. One
of my greatest attributes is knowing when I'm any good and when I'm
not any good. I don't have an inflated or a deflated opinion of myself;
I'm fairly honest and aware of when I've done something well and
when I've done it poorly.

Walter Cronkite was wrong when he accused himself of not being a
very good writer. Cronkite's focus went beyond just the writing.

Actually, I was terribly intent on making the story understandable
and trying to cover as much of the story as we could with the limited
amount of time we had. And I don't think I succeeded greatly in doing
that job, because our philosophy at the moment, my philosophy certainly, was to jam into that twenty-four minutes we had as much news
as we could. So we were really packing the show a little too tight by
compressing as much as we did into those few minutes. We were
doing the same thing you do when you try to put five pounds of gas
into a three-pound container. You create as much explosive force as
you do light. But the point was that in delivering it, I was really intent
that the viewer understand our story. I never thought about how I
looked or how I should gesture or anything else.

Some writers try to avoid it; Cronkite almost pioneered it. It's called
"journalese." It's a style that leans toward the sensational or the cliché.

As I say, with television, my whole thrust was making people
understand it. And that meant, in a sense, restrictive language. A journalese, if you please. We wrote journalese. And a lot of people have
criticized that in me. I've been, I think, demeaned by a lot of colleagues
who think I'm not a writer. And they're right, in a sense. I'm not a fine
writer. I've never pretended to be. I never even wanted to be. I never

had any desire to write a piece of fiction. I never read very much fiction, even. I'm not good at that sort of thing. I'm a fast, accurate news writer. That's my style, and I'm stuck with it."

There are many who wish they could be "stuck" with such a style.

NAMES TO REMEMBER

Isn't it funny how we all seem to remember who our mentors were—where that one nugget of advice came from that influenced our viewpoint and changed the way we did things?

I had a mentor named Al Spiro. I worked for him at a small but tough and influential suburban New York radio station, where I worked my way up to news director and eventually started writing editorials. Spiro gave me the simplest and best advice I ever got about writing. "Think *New York Times*," he said, "but write *Daily News*."

Walter Cronkite developed his keyboard skills while working in the trenches of the rough-and-tumble newswire services.

We had a wonderful overnight editor at the United Press named Allah Smith. He worked here in the *Daily News* building, where the United Press headquarters were at the time. I had the opportunity of being his major reporter/writer/editor in Kansas City, Missouri, which was where the national wire of United Press "broke," we called it, between the East and West coasts. All the West Coast news came into Kansas City; all the East Coast news came into Kansas City. We had to edit down the copy from the East to the West. We had to take the West Coast copy and prepare it for the East. We had a three-hour time difference, of course. Preparing it was, to a great extent, rewriting it. The United Press standards for the East Coast were higher than they were for the West Coast, which meant a lot of rewriting. And so I sat there as an overnight editor in Kansas City. I came in at midnight, took the night wires, and rewrote them for the opening of the wire going on to the East at 3:00 a.m. And Allah Smith was a tough, really tough, editor but a wonderful mentor, and he had his version of "Think *New York Times* and write *Daily News*." His was "Write this so the Kansas City milkman understands it." And he constantly sent copy back with the note, "Where's the KC KP?" KP was the sign of the Kansas City United Press. Meaning that your story needed a rewrite so that the Kansas City milkman could understand it.

Tom Brokaw remembers working for one of his mentors in the South, during the beginnings of the civil rights movement.

I worked for Ray Moore in Atlanta. He was one of the early contemporary broadcast journalists in the South. It was about plain talk with him—about explaining. I remember I went off to cover a group of black students trying to get on a school bus to go integrate another school, and they got pulled off the bus and beaten up by a bunch of rednecks. Then they turned on us, and I was there by myself with just my cameraman and a guy from the AP. It was really a harrowing experience and very dangerous. We were in the middle of nowhere in this little redneck town. And when I came back I was going to write it as a conventional news story, and Ray Moore said, "No. I want you to go on camera tonight and look into the lens and tell this community what you went through. Tell Atlanta what it was like to be a journalist, white, and have the crowd turn on you, so that people will begin to understand what it's like to be young and black during all this."The switchboard lit up. And it was all sympathetic calls, because it was a way of letting people know what it was like to have your rights stripped from you, to have a crowd turn on you, to have no protection. And I said at the end, "So that's what it feels like to be a young black student or civil rights demonstrator—and, I'm telling you, I never thought it would happen in this country."

There was a lesson in all of that for Brokaw.

"It did remind me that there are times when you cannot be just at arm's length from a story. That sometimes the personal experience, conveyed in the proper way, is appropriate journalism."

If Your Mother Tells You
She Loves You, Check It Out!

W hen I retired as an investigative reporter in 1994, colleagues marked the occasion with a terrific party at Gracie Mansion. Mayor Giuliani was there, of course, and former mayor David Dinkins. Linda Hall in *New York Magazine* wrote that my "peers, bosses, competitors, and friends" were all there. They roasted me with comments like, "Art was lazy, Art was erratic. Art's major hobbies were smoking and going to lunch." I loved it.

Linda Hall wrote that "[in Art] delinquency was synonymous with a disregard for stale propriety—and, as Rich Lamb put it, '[he had an] understanding that larceny is always just around the corner from a cathedral, if we're lucky enough not to find it in the pews.'"

Dumb and Dumber? Not Quite

But enough about me. With friends like Jerry Nachman, you get down to earth fast. It was his remarks at my retirement party about the future of journalism that triggered in me the need to write this book. *Were* we more dedicated? *Were* we smarter? What did he think?

I don't think they're stupider than we were coming into this business today. But we knew how dumb we were! We were self-conscious about it and terrified of it. When I walked into News Radio 88 as a writer in April of 1971, I was introduced to the "local" radio guys. They were Charlie Osgood, Dave Marash, and Ed Bradley. And I thought "F—k me! I'm not ready to play in this league! So I did what every reporter for eight hundred years did. I shut up. I listened to what the smart ones were saying. The difference between then and now is that they're so *poised* about how dumb they are.

Because we knew how dumb we were, we made it a point to learn. I remember coming back from City Hall one Sunday morning and standing around Steve Flanders's desk at WCBS with Rich Lamb and Irene Cornell and talking. Andy Haywood, a station exec, came in and chewed us out. "You're wasting an awful lot of money, you people standing around talking." And I said, "We're not just talking. We're learning." And in a remark that crystallized the divide between news management and news talent, he answered, "Well, this isn't the place to learn."

GOT THE GOODS?

But seriously folks, it's probably time to talk about what lessons we've learned from tapping the best acts in the business. Of the wealth of information all my sources were good enough to give me, certain lessons stand out as indispensable for excellent journalism and successful journalists.

First, and without exception: If you are not incurably curious, find something else to do. And once you've gathered the facts of a story you think everyone should hear, check your facts! All of them. Don Hewitt once told me that a Chicago editor told him, "Kid, if your mother tells you she loves you—check it out."

Now, writing skill must come into play. "A story needs to unfold," advises Lynn Sherr. "We don't do the five Ws in the first paragraph like in daily journalism, but . . . I want that 'nut' paragraph in. I like starting with a tease. I like sucking people in. But please say, 'Here are the facts of this story.'"

And avoid clichés like the plague. "I find this in the younger producers," Sherr observes. "They think they have to use every cliché in the book." Sherr's particular pet peeve is the word "tragic." "I will not allow the use of the word 'tragic' in a piece I've done, unless it really *is* tragic. There are horrible accidents. There are gruesome accidents, but not every accident is a tragic accident. Does every death have to be untimely and every killing senseless?"

Find another way to say it! There is always another way to say it. And if you can't find it, no one will hear you.

Once you've got a well-crafted piece, journalistic ethics *must* kick in. Is the piece fair? Is it fact or opinion? And, possibly most important, is it objective? Mike Wallace relates a story of an interview he conducted that made him "genuinely embarrassed." He was interviewing the president of the chemical company involved in the contamination of Love Canal in upstate New York. The man had been gracious enough to agree to be interviewed on air, and he conceded that they had done some things wrong but maintained that they were trying to do things better. Wallace recalls:

> And we went after him, book, chapter, and verse, and it developed into overkill. This was an issue of great importance to the American people at the time—he was the villain and we were going after the villain. I went in as a journalist and took an adversary point of view. But if you're after drama, if you're after heat instead of light . . . you're losing your way.

What lesson did he learn here?

WALLACE: Fairness. Once you've got your story, don't drive it into the ground. Once you have an understanding out of the mouth of the person you are talking to, lay off.

ATHENS: Do you remember the famous Rather-Nixon "live" incident? Do you think Rather was wrong? Did he go too far?

WALLACE: I think both of them went too far. They got caught up in the live drama.

ATHENS: But when you say to the vice president of the United States, "What about this? We think you did this." And he says "No, I didn't." And you say, "Are you sure? Information says you did." And he says, "I'm absolutely sure I didn't." Should you continue to argue with him?

WALLACE: Well, you shouldn't argue with him.

ATHENS: If that's his answer, it should stand?

WALLACE: You shouldn't argue with him, but it's not an argument if you pursue something because you believe you have evidence contrary to what he is saying. In my estimation, neither Rather nor Nixon covered himself in glory. We were looking at a psychodrama rather than reportage—and that's not our role.

And what about balance? How do you make sure you treat both sides of the story evenly when you're up against broadcast deadlines, or when it's impossible to reach the other side? Brian Williams says, "It should be reflexive. It has to be taught when people are starting out, but it should never be something an editor has to order you to do. If it's late-breaking news, the next day you follow with the other side."

STAY OUT OF IT!

Adversary or advocate—both are out of place in journalism. There was a trend in journalism that started in the nineties to become part of the story, to shape it—advocacy journalism, for or against. I don't know where this came from, but it seems to be the case.

Brian Williams has strong feelings here.

> I won't allow the expression "our troops" or "our economy." I won't allow things like "Desert Storm." You might as well do the Pentagon's bidding on the air. I use, instead, "Persian Gulf War." I don't ever speak of the United States as a collective that I am a part of. I am a dispassionate observer.
>
> My wife doesn't know who I voted for in the last election. No one on the planet knows. I guard my opinions with incredible care. I would sooner walk naked out onto a television show than divulge my opinions politically.
>
> Entire families are supported by the opinion business. Young people think that what Sam [Donaldson] and Cokie [Roberts] do is news. It's not. It's opinion. Why have all that baggage to get over every time you begin speaking? Sam Donaldson had to file straight news pieces for a couple of nights, filling in for Brit Hume. Every informed viewer sat at home thinking, "This guy gives very left-leaning opinions on Brinkley every Sunday morning. So cull that out . . . see if there's any attitude.

Now, even after you've tried to be as fair, dispassionate, and objective as possible, how can you be sure you've done it? Well, *you* can't. That's why Williams lets others do that for him.

> Everything I write goes through four sets of eyes before it goes anywhere near a television. I demand a million backstops on my words before they go on the air. I'm about to go to a Christmas party at the

Clintons' house. I got a nice, pretty invitation and we're going to cele-brate Christmas together, and tonight I'm doing a piece on Mrs. Clinton and her plans to get involved in welfare policy. It's going to have to pass muster by those four people.

Charles Kuralt recalls watching a local TV story about a kids' tricycle race,

> a very attractive story about three- and four-year-olds, unpolished in their tricycle skills, doing their best. Halfway through the story, Izzy [his cameraman] said, "You know what? Before this story is over that reporter is going to ride a tricycle." I said, "Oh no, he wouldn't. It would turn into a joke." Sure enough, we get a close-up of the guy and he says, "Joe Doe, Eyewitness News," and they pull back and he turns and rides away, which ruined the whole story. And so we developed the "tricycle principle": Keep yourself out of the story!"

BE CAREFUL WHAT YOU WRITE— YOU MAY HAVE TO READ IT

We've talked a lot in this book about storytelling—about what makes for good storytelling and what will blow it. Just a few final words of advice from the best of the best at this, Charles Kuralt and Charles Osgood. First, Kuralt:

> Simplest is best. Don't use a long word when a short one will suf-fice. And don't take yourself too seriously—that's the biggest, most helpful thing you could tell young people. Don't worry about how you're going to appear in the story. Your job is to be the conveyor of this story to others.

Charles Osgood, who insists you have to sound like yourself and not like somebody else, illustrates with an Ethel Merman anecdote.

> Ethel Merman was in her twenties when the Gershwins were about to put *Girl Crazy* on Broadway, and somebody sent her up to the apartment on Riverside Drive to audition. They asked her to sing

"I Got Rhythm," and Gershwin said, "Where have you been? What have you been doing?" And she said, "Well, I'm taking singing lessons." And Gershwin said, "Stop! Don't take one more lesson. Nobody can sing like you do, and if you take enough lessons, you'll sing like other people."

I traded Osgood one about Bob Newhart, who when he got his first show was supposedly told by the director, "You know, I think this would be a lot funnier show if you'd stop the stammer"—which, of course, turned out to be his trademark.

Begin at the Beginning

Leslie Stahl was at the top of the heap, not once but twice.

I started my career in journalism at NBC News, which for a television reporter was starting at the top. This was a big mistake. After a few years I had to quit and start all over again at the beginning, 'cause I hadn't built the foundation. I went back to local television in Boston; they hired me as a producer and I had to learn the business by doing it. My advice is, go to the place where they give you the beginning job, and start to do it. That's the only way to become a journalist.

When I was a teenager, I used to listen to Jean Shepherd on WOR Radio in New York. Jean was a great storyteller, and his late-night broadcast had a large "cult" following among young people. I used to hide the radio under my pillow to muffle the sound, so my parents wouldn't hear it. I was spellbound. At one in the morning, after Jean's show ended, he had a call-in hour. I was lucky enough to get through to him one night. I told him I wanted to get into the radio business; it was all I ever wanted. Jean's advice was, "Kid, you have to start in Podunk and work your way back." So I did. Years later, after I had worked my way back to WCBS Radio in New York, I met Jean. I had the opportunity to thank him for his advice. It was a great moment for me.

So where *should* you start? Is that place journalism school? Some would agree. But Lynn Sherr is adamant in her belief that you only want to do that as a graduate student.

There are undergraduate journalism professors around the country who hate me, because I always say, learn something: Major in history, botany, biology, economics . . . Hone your skills in school; work for a paper, work for a broadcast. Get the basic knowledge you need to do the proper research and have the right kind of brain.

And if you're lucky enough to land in a good place, Dan Rather's advice is, stay there!

I think people are a little reluctant to stay in one place very long, because somehow the idea has gotten out that the way you get ahead is to keep moving. That wasn't my experience. Once you find a good environment, a good outfit, a good news director, and you have the opportunity to do a lot of different things—even if you get a bigger offer, I might stay where you are. There is something to be said for just staying in one place. Keep plowing that furrow and learning the craft in a good environment.

TO HELL IN A HANDBASKET? NOT IF WE CAN HELP IT!

If I were to take a voice vote now among the journalists I have had the privilege to interview for this book, and I asked them if they thought journalism, as we knew it, had a bright future, I think the nays would have it. But with the against-all-odds drive it takes to succeed in this business, the next thing they would do is take those lemons and give me a recipe for lemonade. And a lot of them did.

BRIAN WILLIAMS: I'm not bullish on the future of our business. The drop-off in the national attention span may mean that only the hungry survive and reach the upper echelons of reporting. But that could be a terrific outcome—there just won't be a market for mediocrity. Stations won't be able to carry ten reporters; they'll have room for only five—and the good ones will survive.

JERRY NACHMAN: There was always a lot of mediocrity. But the business is so hard and so arbitrary, it serves as a disincentive for all but the profoundly motivated. And that's good—it's supposed to be hard. That's why we call it work. Those that really want it will persevere, and they'll get to it.

TOM BROKAW: There are some brilliant young people writing for newspapers these days. Magazines are better than they've ever been in terms of the scope and depth of reporting.

And important things have changed for the better, at least for some. Don Fitzpatrick, a news consultant with years of experience in the business, talks about the gender breakthrough.

> A lot of things have changed. Contrary to what some people say, women have finally come of age, and women can go over forty and they can go over fifty and, in some cases, they can go over sixty and remain on television. But the chances of a woman over forty being able to leave Albuquerque and move to Los Angeles or New York are probably slim to none, simply because so many women have gotten into the business in the last fifteen years. There are younger, smarter women who are hungry, who are willing to fight tooth and nail to get those jobs in L.A., New York, and San Francisco."

And if you think, and many do, that upper management is running the broadcast industry "like a widget factory," are there alternatives short of getting out of the business altogether? All around, the conclusion seems to be, if you can't work with integrity on the major networks, go to cable television or National Public Radio. Brokaw calls NPR a "gift to America." And he has kind words for C-SPAN.

Brian Williams found a temporary home on MSNBC:

> I go home now every night with my held high. I'm doing an hour of news in prime time on a very serious-minded broadcast. My god! I'll never be accused of going where the viewers are. We have a horrifyingly small audience at night. But when you're a niche broadcaster, people who've taken pains to find your broadcast on MSNBC at 9:00 p.m., shunning *Seinfeld*—boy, are they a serious news audience, and they deserve a very serious broadcast.

PBS's Judy Woodruff, Williams recalls, once said, "Remember, one of our viewers is worth eight of theirs."

PERSISTENCE, GUMPTION, AND A BULLETPROOF EGO

You'd better have talent! You'd better have passion! You'd better have drive! And with all that, the pros say, you are still going to need a lot of luck. I asked Mike Wallace, "If you were starting out today, young Mike Wallace, wanting to make his mark, wanting to achieve excellence, how would you go about it?" He responded:

I'd probably go to cable. There's a lot of, pardon the expression, crap on cable, but there's narrowcasting as opposed to broadcasting. Some of the things I see on A&E, on the History Channel, on the Learning Channel . . . I think they are doing an absolutely first-rate job. You may not make as much money if you go to cable. Cable salaries are minuscule compared to some of the commercial news broadcasts. But the psychic income is immense.

One newswoman proved that for her, it was not about the money. Her name is Carol Marin, and she worked in the Chicago market. Don Fitzpatrick told me, "Carol Marin gave up a million-dollar-a-year salary to say, 'I won't allow Jerry Springer to be a commentator on my news broadcast.'"

We are an industry with standards, and the standards police are the Committee for Excellence in Journalism. Its most recent report suggested that the quality of news is no better than it was last year, and that local news, in particular, is very poor. I discussed this issue with Tom Brokaw.

I think there has been a real deterioration in local news. But the fact is, those local news outlets that are trying to raise the bar are succeeding. The grave danger, especially at the local news level, is that it has become duplicative, and you can't distinguish one from the other. So those stations around the country where they say, "We're going to do more investigative reporting, we're going to invest more in City Hall reporting," they're beginning to do better. And I hope that's a trend that will begin to catch on.

LOOKING FORWARD TO THE GOOD OLD DAYS

And what about the good old days? Were they really as good as we like to remember? Tom Brokaw recalls that even when Bill Paley owned CBS, he killed Edward R. Murrow's programs. And Edward R. Murrow did *Person to Person,* and it succeeded because it was commercial. It was the *People* magazine of the air when he was doing it. We tend to have what I call a rose-colored rearview mirror. When we look back, we tend to remember only the best.

He remembers, too, a "sensationalist" incident that landed him, a cub reporter, on the Huntley-Brinkley show on national television.

A woman fell off a sway bar in the circus in town, and there happened to be a still photographer there who was very good, and he got pictures of her on the way down and on the ground. So it became a minute spot, and I was the voice, and I was a kid in Omaha. So that was on Huntley-Brinkley during the so-called halcyon days of news!

I asked Brokaw more generally about journalism's appeal today—to its potential practitioners as well as its younger potential consumers.

ATHENS: If there is a litmus test to determine whether you should go into journalism or not, what would that be? I talked to one young woman who is now working at CBS as a writer, and she's very good, very bright. And I'm impressed that she is only 23 years old. In her college class, only she and two others read the papers and watched or listened to the news.

BROKAW: I'm not surprised. A lot of younger people don't think the news has any relationship to their lives. The *New York Times* is talking about Social Security reform or the Middle East, and they'll say, "What has that got to do with me?" They also have other places to go to get the news—and not just newspapers. They get a hell of a lot of news off the Internet—and they find a lot of news of interest to them.

Dan Rather still believes in the "big leagues." But his big leagues are ones we can all believe in. What he describes is a team we can all play on—every one of us.

What makes them the big leagues, what makes it the big time, is the number of people who are striving every day for excellence. That's what makes the big time. It doesn't get easier the higher you go, it gets tougher—but what gets better is the sense that you are working shoulder to shoulder with people who are striving for excellence.

And that's the truth.

EPILOGUE

Art Athens died finishing this book. He labored three years on it. He was trying to beat what he could not have known would be his final deadline.

Art's magnetic personality brought him a universe of friends, colleagues, and listeners. He could tell a stem-winder of a story with a fabric and texture so fascinating you wanted to drop what you were doing to listen—and you often did. You were hooked, trapped, transfixed. His intellect would find "a puzzle wrapped in a mystery surrounded by an enigma" explainable—just another entertaining challenge to put into words. He made the complex simple, and he could tell a complicated tale flawlessly, with the precision of a university professor and the timing of a comic master. Athens's facile mind could grasp the basics of any story. His two typing fingers would then reach to the keyboard and "pound home" a connection to the human mind and heart. He could relate an otherwise dry and unappealing city budget story to your house, to your street, and to you.

As Art says so powerfully in this book, journalism seemed to have chosen *him*. Among his New York reporter colleagues he was a force of nature, the "perfect storm" of radio reporting. His hallmark was the consistent excellence of his work. Listeners loved him. Colleagues were in awe of him. On the day he left CBS I took a look inside his office: Twenty-one hooks on the wall held major awards.

Art saw himself as a reporter in the trenches, a correspondent—but also as a mentor, and as a "keeper of the flame" of journalism. He would rant and rave about poor reporting, murderous English usage, incorrect grammar, clumsy syntax, and content errors. He loved news, made clear what it meant to him, and embraced its practitioners and their audience. His heroes were the great names in the news business. He stuck relentlessly to the standards they had established.

This book shows how deeply rooted was his conviction that broadcast journalism has a pivotal role to play in our democracy, and that we in journalism should strive for the sometimes elusive but always worthy holy grails of balance and truth. He wanted journalism's banner carried proudly and had no patience for anyone who would sully it.

But this tough, streetwise, competitive, laser-focused reporter had a very funny, zany side. His bottomless well of humor included thousands of jokes, each of which he told with exacting technique, hilarious accents, and matchless style. He refused to accept anyone's bad mood, pummeling any grumbler with jokes and one-liners until the lemon-pussed reporter or anchor had to laugh. He was a serious reporter who never took himself too seriously.

Art's office at the otherwise staid CBS headquarters building displayed his personality. The emblem of his space was a sign: It said, simply, "A neat desk is a sign of a sick mind." Featured prominently on one wall was a poster depicting a "rear view" of a man wearing only a raincoat, held wide open in front of a marble statue. The caption read, "Expose yourself to Art." Also in his office was a Rudy Giuliani–autographed yellow rubber duck accompanied by two yellow rubber chickens hanging from an upturned, brown, magnetized imitation deer foot. Another sign hung on the front of Art's desk. It came from a polling place somewhere in upstate New York and read, "Sign in here. If you are blind or disabled or unable to read or write, you may receive assistance in the voting booth."

Without a doubt, this book is Art's crowning achievement. In it he has taken us into the minds of some of the greats of broadcast journalism. His access to those on the Mount Rushmore of the news business, made possible by his charming, affable style and dauntless persistence, unlocks doors rarely if ever-before opened. As usual, Art has produced something that has taken all of us "to the next level": from the venerable Walter Cronkite's decision to get into the business based on a cartoon and a high school journalism class, to a riveting discussion of real-world news ethics by Dan Rather, Mike Wallace, Andy Rooney, Linda Ellerbee, and Tom Brokaw. Should newspeople do commercials? What's the story process at *60 Minutes?* Why not quit or be fired once in a while?

In this book, Art has single-handedly cut a path through a dark and otherwise confusing jungle of misinformation to the mother lode of broadcast journalism's infrequently mentioned secrets. Along the way, with characteristic subtlety, he has pounded in signposts, not unlike the old Burma Shave signs, containing great war stories from Don Hewitt, Charles Kuralt, Charles Osgood, Lynn Sherr, and Ed Bradley, among others.

The great disappointment is that Art is gone. We cannot thank him. The heart disease and diabetes he battled for twenty years finally claimed him. My regret is that I cannot tell him in person of the singular legacy he has left us in the thinking, standards, and musings set forth here.

I can see him now in our old office at Black Rock in midtown Manhattan. The phrase he used more than any other over the years we worked together was "Hey, got a minute?" Art would play a tape he had just done. He loved a story filled with emotions. It might be a veteran describing a life shattered by Vietnam, or an immigrant sending a chill up your spine describing her foggy first vision of the Statue of Liberty. In the silence after the tape ended, Art and I would look at each other. Tears might brim. The piece met the test if neither of us was able to speak for a few seconds. Art was a reporter who cared right down to the very fiber of his being about what he did. It is an understatement to say that he did it extraordinarily well.

In his tribute at Art's memorial service, New York University Professor Mike Ludlum, also a former news director at WCBS, said he has learned that some people are irreplaceable, and that Art Athens was one of them. If you've read this book, and felt Art's intelligence, warmth, and wit, you'll likely agree.

I'll miss his brilliant analysis, his light touch with weighty issues, his impatience with pomposity. His life was an exercise in enlightened curiosity. He would find an angle from which the world might never before have been examined, then put it into words on the radio in his unique, compelling voice.

Charles Kuralt once described the word "unique" by saying, "Unique stands alone in the universe, unable to be modified." Art was unique. His abilities in this business in some ways did make him stand alone. But wherever he now is in the universe, I believe he has an audience.

—RICH LAMB, WCBS RADIO

CONTRIBUTORS

≈

ED BRADLEY

In 2000, Ed Bradley celebrated his nineteenth season as co-editor of and correspondent for *60 Minutes*. His more notable reports for *60 Minutes* have included "Big Man, Big Voice," the uplifting story of a German singer who became successful despite birth defects; a report on the cruel effects of nuclear testing on the town of Semipalatinsk, Kazakhstan; and "Schizophrenia," a report on that misunderstood brain disorder.

Bradley also reports for primetime specials. "Unsafe Haven" for *60 Minutes II* made headlines by exposing unsafe training methods and poorly trained workers inside the nation's largest chain of psychiatric hospitals. "Town under Siege," a report about a small town battling the oil industry over toxic waste, was hailed as one of the ten best television programs of 1997 by *Time* magazine. He covered presidential campaigns and national conventions from 1976 through 1996 for CBS.

Before joining *60 Minutes* Bradley was principal correspondent for *CBS Reports*, a CBS News White House correspondent, anchor of the *CBS Sunday Night News*, and anchor of that network's *Street Stories*. He joined CBS News as a stringer in its Paris bureau in 1971 and was transferred to the Saigon bureau a year later. He was named CBS News correspondent in 1973 and, shortly thereafter, was wounded on assignment in Cambodia. He was assigned to the CBS Washington bureau in 1974 and volunteered in 1975 to return to Indochina, where he covered the fall of Cambodia and Vietnam.

Prior to joining CBS News, Bradley was a reporter for WCBS Radio in New York. He had previously been a reporter for WDAS Radio in Philadelphia.

Bradley has been awarded eleven Emmys, the Overseas Press Club Award, and the Alfred I. duPont–Columbia University Silver Baton, among others. Bradley's coverage of the plight of Cambodian refugees, broadcast on the *CBS Evening News with Walter Cronkite* and *CBS News Sunday Morning*, won a George Polk Award in journalism.

TOM BROKAW

Tom Brokaw is the anchor and managing editor of *NBC Nightly News with Tom Brokaw*, a contributing editor to *Dateline NBC*, and a program anchor for MSNBC. Equally at ease covering news events from the world's capitals or from small-town America, he has an impressive list of "firsts" to his credit. He conducted the first exclusive one-on-one interview in the United States with Mikhail Gorbachev, for which he won an Alfred I. duPont–Columbia University Award. He was the only anchor to report from the scene the night the Berlin Wall fell. He was the first American anchor to report on the human rights abuses in Tibet and to interview the Dalai Lama.

Brokaw was also the first to report from the site of the Oklahoma City bombing in 1995 and the TWA Flight 800 tragedy in 1996. He was the anchor who found and interviewed Charlie Trie and Johnny Chung, key figures in the 1997 campaign finance abuse scandal. He was the first network anchor to travel to Albania during the NATO air strikes in Yugoslavia. He conducted the first U.S. television interview with the newly installed Russian president Vladimir Putin. He also served as master of ceremonies for the opening of the National D-Day Museum on the fifty-sixth anniversary of the Normandy invasion.

His work before *Nightly News* included the *Brokaw Report* (1992–1993) and *Now with Tom Brokaw and Katie Couric* (1993–1994). Among his many awards were an Alfred I. duPont–Columbia University Award for the documentary special "Why Can't We Live Together," examining racial separation in America's suburbs; a Peabody Award for "To Be an American"; and an Emmy for his "China in Crisis" special.

Brokaw was inducted into the Broadcasting and Cable TV Hall of Fame in 1997 and received a Congressional Medal of Honor in 1999. Complementing his distinguished broadcast journalism career, Brokaw has written articles, essays, and commentary for the *New York Times*, the *Washington Post*, the *Los Angeles Times*, *Newsweek*, and others. He published his first book in 1998, entitled *The Greatest Generation*. A bestseller, the book follows the generation of Americans born in the 1920s who came of age during the Great Depression, fought in World War II, and went on to build America. His second book, *The Greatest Generation Speaks*, was published in 1999.

Brokaw has received numerous honorary degrees, from Notre Dame,

Duke University, Boston College, and the University of Pennsylvania. In 1997, NBC established the Tom Brokaw Scholarship Program in commemoration of his thirty years of service. It provides scholarship support to children of NBC employees pursuing higher education.

Brokaw joined NBC News in 1966, reporting from California and anchoring for KNBC, its Los Angeles affiliate. He has served as NBC's White House correspondent and anchor of NBC News's *Today*, and he has covered every presidential election since 1968. Brokaw began his career in journalism in 1962 at KMTV in Omaha. In 1965, he anchored the late-evening news on WSB-TV in Atlanta.

WALTER CRONKITE

Walter Cronkite has covered virtually every news event during his more than sixty years in journalism, the last fifty spent in association with CBS News. He became a special correspondent for CBS News when he stepped down on March 6, 1981, after nineteen years as anchor and managing editor of the *CBS Evening News*. Cronkite's accomplishments have won him the acclaim and trust of journalism colleagues and the American public alike.

Cronkite began his career in journalism as a campus correspondent for the *Houston Post*. He also worked as a sports announcer for a local radio station in Oklahoma City. He joined United Press in 1937 and remained there for eleven years. As a UP correspondent he covered World War II, landing with the invading Allied troops in North Africa, covering the battle of the North Atlantic, and taking part in the Normandy beachhead assaults and the B-17 raids over Germany. After reporting the German surrender, Cronkite established the United Press bureaus in Europe and was named bureau chief in Brussels, whence he covered the Nuremberg trials. From 1946 to 1948, he was chief correspondent in Moscow.

In 1950 Cronkite joined CBS News in Washington as a correspondent and anchored most political convention and election coverage from 1952 to 1980. He assumed his duties on the *CBS Evening News* in 1962 as anchor of a fifteen-minute broadcast. In 1963 the program became network television's first half-hour weeknight broadcast, inaugurated with Cronkite's headline-making interview with President John F. Kennedy.

When he stepped down in 1981, Cronkite became a special correspondent for CBS News and hosted several acclaimed documentaries. These included the Emmy-winning "Children of Apartheid" and the CBS News science magazine series *Walter Cronkite's Universe.* He continues to host many public affairs and cultural programs for PBS and syndication, including more than forty award-winning documentary hours for the Discovery Channel and other networks. His production company, the Cronkite Ward Company, produced his memoirs, entitled *Cronkite Remembers.*

In 1985 Cronkite was inducted into the Academy of Television Arts and Sciences Hall of Fame. He was the only journalist to be voted among the top ten "most influential decision makers in America" in surveys conducted by *U. S. News and World Report.* He was also named the most "influential person in broadcasting." In 1995, more than a decade after leaving his CBS anchor desk, he was again voted "the most trusted man in television news."

Cronkite is an avid sailor; he recorded his experiences sailing his sixty-foot yacht from Chesapeake Bay to Key West in his book *South by Southeast. North by Northeast* covered his sailing experiences in that region, and *Westwind* recounted his sailing tour of America's West Coast. His first book, *Eye on the World,* was an edited compendium of CBS News's reporting on major trends and stories of 1970. His autobiography, *A Reporter's Life,* was published by Knopf.

LINDA ELLERBEE

Linda Ellerbee is an outspoken journalist, an award-winning television producer, a best-selling author, one of the most sought-after speakers in America, a breast cancer survivor, and a mom.

Ellerbee began at CBS and then moved to NBC News—where, after covering politics, she cultivated a diverse following in the 1980s with the pioneering late-night news program *NBC News Overnight,* which she wrote and co-anchored. *Overnight* was cited by the duPont–Columbia Award it received as "the best written and most intelligent news program ever." In 1986 Ellerbee moved to ABC News to anchor and write *Our World,* a weekly prime-time historical series. Her work on *Our World* won her an Emmy for best writing.

In 1987, Ellerbee and her partner, Rolfe Tessem, quit the network to start Lucky Duck Productions, initially producing documentaries for

PBS. In 1991, Lucky Duck began producing—with Ellerbee writing and hosting—*Nick News*. Nine years later, *Nick News*, which airs on Nickelodeon and on close to two hundred stations in syndication, is the most popular children's news program on television and one of the most acclaimed children's programs of any kind. *Nick News* has collected three Peabody Awards (including one personal Peabody given to Ellerbee for her coverage of the Clinton investigation), a duPont–Columbia Award, and two Emmys.

Lucky Duck currently produces prime-time specials for HBO, Lifetime, MSNBC, A&E, MTV, ABC, CBS, and Nickelodeon. Lucky Duck is also one of the premiere producers of the weekly *Intimate Portrait* series for Lifetime Television, and of *Headliners and Legends with Matt Lauer* for MSNBC. Recently, HBO signed Ellerbee, Whoopi Goldberg, and Diane Keaton to develop a twelve-hour mini-series about the women's movement of the 1960s and 1970s.

The first two books of Ellerbee's eight-part series for middle-school children, entitled *Get Real*, hit the bookshelves in March of 2000; new titles continued to be released every other month through 2001. Her first book, *And So It Goes*, a humorous look at television news, is used as a textbook in more than one hundred colleges across the country. Ellerbee's second bestseller, *Move On*, is a candid look at her life as a working single mother trying to find balance in her life.

As a breast cancer survivor, Ellerbee travels thousands of miles each year giving inspirational speeches to others. Although she has won television's highest honors, she says her two children have brought her her richest rewards.

Don Hewitt

Don Hewitt was the creator of *60 Minutes* and its Executive Producer from its CBS debut in 1968 to May of 2004, when he became an Executive Producer at CBS News. He joined CBS News in 1948 as associate director of the first network newscast, *Douglas Edwards and the News*. In the 1950s he directed the breakthrough public affairs program *See It Now* with Edward R. Murrow. Hewitt was the first to use two film projectors, cutting back and forth to break up the monotony of "talking heads," along with cue cards for his "anchor," an enduring term he coined to describe Walter Cronkite's new role at political conventions.

Highlights of Hewitt's earlier work included direction and production of a television documentary on the coronation of Queen Elizabeth. Flying over the Atlantic in 1956, he got the only footage of the sinking of the *Andrea Doria* just before it disappeared. He directed and produced the first televised presidential debate, between John F. Kennedy and Richard Nixon, in 1960. He put CBS News's coverage of the early space launches on a screen in New York City's Grand Central Station. In 1963 he became the executive producer of *The CBS Evening News with Walter Cronkite*, the first network half-hour newscast, and he moved on two years later to head CBS's documentary unit.

In 1967 he invented the "news magazine" format when he created *60 Minutes*, with Mike Wallace as co-editor. *60 Minutes* got its present time slot from 7:00 to 8:00 p.m. on Sundays in 1976, and it had finished in the Nielsen top twenty by 1978; it has remained there ever since. In 1993 the program won the number-one Nielsen slot, the only program to have done so in three separate decades.

Don Hewitt has received numerous awards for his involvement with *60 Minutes*, among them a "Founders Emmy" from the International Council of the National Academy of Arts and Sciences, the "Presidential Award for Lifetime Achievement" from the Overseas Press Club, and two First Amendment awards, the Committee to Protect Journalists's Burton Benjamin Memorial Award for press freedom and the Spirit of Liberty Award from the People for the American Way Foundation.

Born in 1922, Hewitt began his journalism career as a copy boy for the *New York Herald Tribune* in 1942, and he became in that same year the youngest war correspondent assigned to General Dwight D. Eisenhower's headquarters, covering the North Atlantic, the North Sea, D-Day, and the Pacific theater. Before joining CBS in 1948 he was a night editor for the Associated Press in Memphis, Tennessee; editor of the *Pelham Sun* in New York; and photo editor for Acme News Pictures, a division of United Press International.

CHARLES KURALT

Charles Kuralt anchored *CBS News Sunday Morning* from its premiere broadcast on January 28, 1979. *Sunday Morning*, which continues with Charles Osgood at the helm, is a weekly tribute to man's accomplishments and achievements: a journey through the worlds of fine art, music, nature, environment, sports, science, and Americana.

In addition to his role on *Sunday Morning*, Kuralt spent much of his career anchoring segments for "On the Road," for which he often wandered along the rural byways and small towns of America. Kuralt set out to see the country in 1967. He and his crew, traveling in a battered motor home, visited every state and logged more than a million miles. "On the Road" served as the final segment of the *CBS Nightly News with Walter Cronkite*.

Kuralt regularly took part in CBS news coverage of special events, such as national elections and the 1989 democracy movement in China. He served as co-host with General Norman Schwartzkopf of a series of CBS News World War II fiftieth-anniversary specials, among them "Remember Pearl Harbor," "The Year of the Generals," and "Hitler and Stalin." During the Persian Gulf War, he and Leslie Stahl co-anchored a late-night CBS News broadcast, *America Tonight*.

In his early years at CBS News, Kuralt reported from far corners of the world: Africa, Asia, and all twenty-three Latin-American nations. Once he spent eight weeks on the ice of the Arctic Ocean covering the attempt of a Polar expedition to reach the North Pole. Kuralt joined CBS in 1957 as a 22-year-old radio writer on the overnight news desk. He became a writer for Douglas Edwards and in 1958 was elevated to reporter on the news assignment desk. In 1959, at age 25, Kuralt became the youngest-ever CBS news correspondent; he later became the first host of the CBS News primetime series *Eyewitness*. In 1961 he was named Latin American correspondent, based in Rio de Janeiro. In 1963 he became chief West Coast correspondent for CBS; he returned to CBS headquarters in New York City the following year. Soon after, he began his travels of back roads largely unexplored by television news. He interrupted his journey in 1980 and 1981 to anchor *Morning with Charles Kuralt* on weekday mornings, and to briefly co-anchor *Morning with Charles Kuralt and Diane Sawyer*.

Kuralt began his journalism career as a columnist for the Charlotte News in his home state of North Carolina—where, just one year later, he won the Ernie Pyle Award. For his work on *Sunday Morning* and "On the Road," Kuralt earned such prestigious honors as three George Foster

Peabody awards and eleven Emmy awards, including a sports Emmy award for his reports from the 1992 Olympic Winter Games in Albertville, France. In 1983, the International Radio and Television Society named Kuralt Broadcaster of the Year. *Time* magazine described him as the "laureate of the common man."

Kuralt detailed his wanderings in six books, including his memoir *A Life on the Road*, which became the best-selling hardcover nonfiction book of 1990. He died in 1997.

JERRY NACHMAN

Jerry Nachman's career spanned radio, television, and print. He worked in front of the camera and behind; on the street, in the newsroom, and in the front office. Nachman served as news director for WNBC-TV in New York City, as vice president of news for WCBS-TV in New York, and as editor-in-chief of the *New York Post*. He also served for many years as an on-air street reporter for both WCBS Radio and WCBS Television in New York; he was a columnist for the *New York Post*; and he served as vice president and general manager of WRC Radio and WRC Television, both NBC-owned properties in Washington, D.C.

More recently, Nachman was employed as a staff writer on *UC: Undercover*, a primetime drama that aired Sunday nights on NBC in late 2001. Nachman also worked as a staff writer on *Politically Incorrect with Bill Maher*, returning in Election Year 2000 as executive producer. He also co-anchored the nightly public affairs broadcast *Life and Times Tonight* at KCET, the Los Angeles PBS station. In addition, Nachman co-wrote a short film for the American Film Institute that won the 1999 Academy Award in the student competition. His final assignment for MSNBC was reporting on the Michael Jackson case in California.

Nachman was the recipient of the prestigious Peabody Award, an Edward R. Murrow Award from the Radio-Television News Directors Association, and an Emmy Award, along with numerous others. He served twice as a Pulitzer Prize juror in the journalism competition.

Nachman concluded his career as vice president and editor-in-chief of MSNBC; he was still serving in that position when he died from cancer, at the age of 57, in 2004. "Jerry Nachman will be remembered not only for what he brought to the news—insight, context, and a relentless search for the truth—but also for what he brought to the newsroom: integrity, tenacity, and a refreshing splash of humor," said NBC News president Neal Shapiro. "His passion for news," observed Erik Sorenson, MSNBC president and general manager, "was contagious."

CHARLES OSGOOD

Charles Osgood is the anchor of *CBS News Sunday Morning* and of "The Osgood File" for CBS Radio. Dubbed the CBS News "poet in residence," he has anchored *Sunday Morning* since 1994. Osgood has anchored and reported for CBS Morning News, *The CBS Evening News with Dan Rather*, and the *CBS Nightly News*. Before joining CBS News in 1971, he was an anchor/reporter for WCBS News Radio 88 in New York City. Prior to that, he was on assignment for ABC News, and he also served as general manager of the first pay television station in the United States, WHCT in Hartford, Connecticut.

In 1990, Osgood was inducted into the National Association of Broadcasters Hall of Fame. He has received an International Radio and Television Society Foundation award and three Peabody Awards. In 1997 he received his third Emmy for his interview on *Sunday Morning* with American realist painter Andrew Wyeth. "The Osgood File" has earned him five coveted *Washington Journalism Review* Best in the Business Awards. Osgood received a 1999 Radio Mercury Award, a 1996 American Society of Composers, Authors, and Publishers President's Award for outstanding coverage and support of music creators, and a 1993 Marconi Radio Award.

Osgood is the author of numerous books. *Nothing Could Be Finer than a Crisis That Is Minor in the Morning* and *There's Nothing I Wouldn't Do if You Would Be My POSSLQ* are compilations of some of his best radio broadcasts, and *The Osgood Files* was a compilation of his newspaper columns. *Osgood on Speaking: How to Think on Your Feet without Falling on Your Face* is a tongue-in-cheek guide to public speaking. Osgood also wrote *See You on the Radio* and *More of See You on the Radio* and edited *Kilroy Was Here: The Best American Humor from World War II* and *Funny Letters From Famous People*. His most recent book, published in 2004, is *Defending Baltimore against Enemy Attack: A Boyhood Year during WWII*.

DAN RATHER

Dan Rather is anchor and managing editor of the *The CBS Evening News*, served as anchor of *48 Hours* for almost fifteen years, and is a correspondent for *60 Minutes II*. Since 1962, when Rather joined CBS News, he has handled some of the most challenging assignments in journalism. His commitment to substantive, fair, and accurate news reporting and his tough, active style have earned him a position of respect among his peers.

Since the start of his career in 1950, Dan Rather has been in the middle of the world's defining moments. From November 22, 1963, in Dallas, when he broke the news of the assassination of President John F. Kennedy, to the 1968 Democratic National Convention, to Beijing, Bosnia, and Hong Kong more than two decades later, he has covered the major news stories. His reporting on the civil rights movement in the South; the White House; the wars in Vietnam, Afghanistan, the Persian Gulf, and Yugoslavia; and the quests for peace in South Africa and the Middle East has showcased his combination of street smarts and acute analysis.

Rather has anchored *The CBS Evening News* since 1981. His regular contributions to CBS News Radio include "Dan Rather Reporting," a weekly broadcast of news and analysis. He joined CBS News as chief of its Southwest bureau in Dallas in 1962; the following year he was made chief of the Southern bureau, responsible for coverage of events in the South, the Southwest, Mexico, and Central America. He began his career in journalism in 1950 as an Associated Press reporter in Huntsville, Texas; later, he reported for United Press International, KSAM Radio in Huntsville, KTRH Radio in Houston, and the *Houston Chronicle*. Prior to joining CBS News, Rather was news director for KHOU-TV, the CBS affiliate in Houston.

Dan Rather has received virtually every honor in broadcast journalism, including numerous Emmys, a Peabody Award, and citations from critical, scholarly, professional, and charitable organizations. His book *Deadlines and Datelines*, a compilation of essays written for his daily radio commentary and weekly syndicated column, was a *New York Times* bestseller, marking the third time that his books have achieved this status; *American Dream: Stories from the Heart of Our Nation* is his most recent book.

ANDY ROONEY

"The most felicitous nonfiction writer in television" is how *Time* magazine once described Andy Rooney, the CBS News correspondent, writer, and producer, who has won the Writer's Guild Award for Best Script of the Year six times, more than any other writer in the history of the medium. Rooney wrote "An Essay on Doors," the first of what has become his specialty, the television essay—a personal format allowing him to illuminate subjects most people take for granted—in 1964.

The 2003–2004 season was his twenty-sixth on *60 Minutes*. His unique reports, "A Few Minutes with Andy Rooney," became a regular feature in 1978; he won Emmys for these essays in 1979, 1981, and 1982. Rooney has done over seven hundred segments for *60 Minutes*.

In addition to his contributions to *60 Minutes*, Rooney wrote, produced, and narrated a series of broadcasts on various aspects of America and American life, including *Andy Rooney Takes Off, Andy Rooney Goes to Work, Andy Rooney Goes to Dinner,* and *Andy Rooney Goes to Washington,* for which he won a Peabody Award. He also participated in CBS News's extensive coverage of the fiftieth anniversary of D-Day by reporting for *CBS News Sunday Morning* on D-Day veterans en route to France aboard the *Queen Elizabeth II*.

Between 1962 and 1968 he collaborated with the late CBS News correspondent Harry Reasoner—Rooney writing and producing, Reasoner narrating—on such notable CBS News specials as *An Essay on Bridges, An Essay on Hotels, An Essay on Women, An Essay on Chairs,* and *The Strange Case of the English Language. An Essay on War* won Rooney his third Writer's Guild Award. His script for *Black History: Lost, Stolen or Strayed* won him his first Emmy Award.

Rooney wrote for *The Garry Moore Show* on the CBS Radio Network and was a writer for Arthur Godfrey. He also wrote for such CBS public affairs broadcasts as *The Twentieth Century, News of America, Adventure, Calendar,* and *The Morning Show.*

Rooney is the author of numerous books; his most recent were *Years of Minutes and Common Nonsense. The Story of the Stars and Stripes,* which he wrote after three years as a correspondent for *Stars and Stripes* in the European theater, was purchased by Metro-Goldwyn-Mayer. Rooney writes a biweekly column for Tribune Media Services which appears in 150 newspapers. He also has contributed articles to *Esquire,*

Life, Look, Reader's Digest, Harper's, Playboy, Saturday Review, Fine Woodworking, and other magazines.

Born in Albany, New York, Rooney was one of only eight correspondents who flew with the Eighth Air Force on the first American bombing raid on Germany.

LYNN SHERR

Lynn Sherr is a correspondent for the ABC Evening News magazine *20/20*; she joined the program in 1986. Across her career, she has been responsible for a wide range of stories and investigative reports, specializing in women's issues and social change.

Among her more notable contributions to *20/20* were an investigation into the military cover-up during the Persian Gulf War, a moving story on plastic surgeons donating their services to battered women, an eye-opening report on the effect of breast size on women's personalities, an hour-long story on alternative treatments for eating disorders, a piece on children who lost their lives in the Oklahoma City Federal Building bombing, and an examination of the way men and women communicate differently in the workplace. She has covered political conventions, reported on Space Shuttle flights, and obtained the only interview with astronaut Sally Ride, a member of the Rogers Commission investigating the explosion of the space shuttle *Challenger.*

Before joining *20/20*, Sherr was both a national and general assignment correspondent for ABC News. She reported on the Claus von Bulow trial and the American hostage situation in Iran.

A celebrated journalist, Lynn Sherr has received two American Women in Radio and Television Commendation Awards, a Peabody, an award from the British Medical Association, a Front Page Award for a report on the dangers of tattooed cosmetics, a Silver Screen Award for a story about a young man dying of AIDS, and an Emmy for a 1980 post-election *Nightline* special, to name just a few.

Sherr has also served as a correspondent for WCBS-TV and for PBS stations WNET in New York and WETA in Washington, D.C. She was anchor for the weekly PBS magazine *USA: People and Politics*; she has also hosted the *MacNeil/Lehrer Report* for PBS. Before her work with WCBS, Sherr was a reporter and writer for the Associated Press in New

York and a reporter and editor for Condé Nast Publications.

She is author of *Failure Is Impossible: Susan B. Anthony in Her Own Words* and ten editions of *The Women's Calendar;* her most recent books are *America the Beautiful: The Stirring True Story behind Our Nation's Favorite Song* and *Tall Blondes: A Book about Giraffes,* which offered a highly praised look at one of our most endearing but little-understood animals. She has also written articles for publications such as the *New York Times,* the *New York Times Book Review, Saturday Review, Ms., Family Circle,* and *Mademoiselle.*

Leslie Stahl

Lesley Stahl has been co-editor of and correspondent for *60 Minutes* since 1991. Before joining *60 Minutes* she served as a CBS News correspondent during the Carter, Reagan, and Bush presidencies. Her reports appeared frequently on *The CBS Evening News,* first with Walter Cronkite, then with Dan Rather. She also served as moderator of *Face the Nation,* CBS News's Sunday-morning public affairs program; in that capacity, she interviewed newsmakers like Margaret Thatcher, Boris Yeltsin, Yassir Arafat, and top U.S. officials. In 1990 she joined Charles Kuralt as co-anchor of *America Tonight,* a late-night CBS News program of interviews and essays.

Stahl covered the Watergate scandal, the attempt on President Ronald Reagan's life, and the Persian Gulf War. She has reported on every United States–Soviet summit since 1979, and on every national political convention and election night since 1974. She anchored several CBS News documentaries, including *The Politics of Cancer* and *In-the-Red Blues,* about the budget deficit.

Stahl has won Emmys for her interviews on *Face the Nation* and *60 Minutes;* one of these honored her for "How We Won the War," a piece about former FDA Commissioner David Kessler's battle with the tobacco industry. She received the Alfred I. duPont–Columbia University Journalism Award for her *60 Minutes* report "Punishing Saddam," which exposed the plight of Iraqi citizens suffering the effects of United Nations sanctions. She was awarded the Fred Friendly First Amendment Award and was recognized by the Radio and Television News Directors Association with an Edward R. Murrow Award for her reports on the

Michigan Militia. In 1990 she was honored with the Dennis Kauff Journalism Award for lifetime achievement in the news profession.

Lesley Stahl's experience covering Washington for over twenty years became the subject of her book *Reporting Live*, published by Simon & Schuster in 1999.

MIKE WALLACE

Mike Wallace has been co-editor of and correspondent for *60 minutes* since its premiere in 1968. At the age of 85, Wallace shows no signs of slowing down. Among his journalistic achievements of the past few years was an exclusive interview with John Nash, the mentally ill genius on whom the movie *A Beautiful Mind* was based. He arranged for a joint interview on *60 Minutes* with Louis Farrakhan and the eldest daughter of Malcolm X, who had accused Farrakhan of indirect complicity in her father's assassination; the broadcast, in May of 2000, made news when Farrakhan admitted that his words might have egged on the assassins.

In 1998 Wallace not only renewed his CBS contract but also enjoyed one of the biggest scoops of the year: He was the only reporter accompanying U.N. Secretary General Kofi Annan to Iraq on his mission to prevent war with Saddam Hussein. His exclusive interview with Annan was broadcast on *60 Minutes* in 1998. His controversial *60 Minutes* program on Dr. Jack Kevorkian in November of that year, in which the show broadcast Kevorkian's own videotape showing him injecting lethal drugs into a terminally ill man, inspired weeks of debate and media coverage. Wallace's no-holds-barred interviewing technique and enterprising reportage are well known, and his numerous interviews include newsmakers both famous and infamous.

Wallace's experiences as a newsman date back to the 1940s, when he was a radio newswriter and broadcaster for the *Chicago Sun*. After serving as a naval communications officer during World War II, he became a news reporter for WMAQ in Chicago. He joined CBS in 1951, left the network in 1955, and returned in 1963, when he was named CBS News correspondent. His television credits include *Night Beat*, *The Mike Wallace Interview*, and *Biography*, focusing on figures from Mao Zedong to Babe Ruth. Wallace covered the war in Vietnam from the front, and he anchored the CBS News/*Washington Post*/*Newsweek* co-production

Watergate: The Secret Story, marking the twentieth anniversary of the break-in at the Watergate complex.

His awards, far too numerous to list here, include a Robert F. Kennedy Journalism Award, nineteen Emmys, three Alfed I. duPont–Columbia University Awards, and three Peabodys. In 1991, he was inducted into the Television Academy Hall of Fame.

Mike Wallace has been awarded honorary doctorates from the University of Massachusetts, the University of Michigan, and the University of Pennsylvania. His books include *Mike Wallace Asks,* a compilation of interviews, and *Close Encounter,* co-authored with Gary Paul Gates.

BRIAN WILLIAMS

Brian Williams is Tom Brokaw's designated successor as anchor of *NBC Nightly News,* which he began anchoring on December 2, 2004, and for which he has been the regular substitute anchor for more than ten years. For seven years he was anchor and managing editor of MSNBC's and CNBC's *The News with Brian Williams,* which became a news pioneer, combining in-depth coverage of the hard news of the day, interviews with the world's newsmakers, and a first-hand look at the next morning's headlines.

From 1994 to 1996, Williams served as NBC's chief White House correspondent. He also anchored the Saturday edition of *NBC Nightly News* for six years.

Williams has reported on numerous stories of national and international importance. In 1997 he provided continuous coverage of the death of Princess Diana for MSNBC, which was simulcast on NBC worldwide. Millions watched his many hours of live coverage following the crash of TWA Flight 800 and his coverage of the death of John F. Kennedy, Jr. As part of NBC News's special election coverage in 1996, Williams took his program to a different city every night to report live on the Clinton and Dole campaigns. He covered the historic election of Nelson Mandela in South Africa, the Arafat-Rabin Mideast peace agreement from Jericho and Jerusalem, and the fiftieth anniversary of the Normandy invasion; he also reported from Haiti prior to the United States invasion. He was the only television news correspondent to accompany Presidents Clinton,

Bush, and Carter to the funeral of Yitzhak Rabin.

Prior to joining NBC News, Williams spent seven years at WCBS-TV in New York, where he won two Emmy awards for his coverage of the 1987 stock market crash and the collapse of the Berlin Wall. He received two other Emmys for his NBC coverage of the Iowa flood in 1993 and for his coverage of the California earthquakes. Before joining WCBS, he worked for WCAU-TV in Philadelphia and WTTG-TV in Washington, D.C. He began his broadcast career in Pittsburgh, Kansas.

INDEX

≈